A FAITH Interrupted

A FAITH Interrupted

An Honest Conversation with
Alienated Catholics

Alice L. Camille & Joel Schorn

LOYOLAPRESS.

CHICAGO

LOYOLAPRESS.
3441 N. ASHLAND AVENUE
CHICAGO, ILLINOIS 60657
(800) 621-1008
WWW.LOYOLABOOKS.ORG

Cover and interior design by Arc Group Ltd

Library of Congress Cataloging-in-Publication Data
Camille, Alice L.
  A faith interrupted : an honest conversation with alienated Catholics / Alice Camille and Joel Schorn.
    p. cm.
  ISBN 0-8294-1682-X
  1. Church work with ex-church members—Catholic Church. 2. Catholic Church—Membership. I. Schorn, Joel. II. Title.
BX2347.8.E82C36 2004
282—dc22

                                                              2004012672

Printed in the United States of America
04 05 06 07 08 Bang 10 9 8 7 6 5 4 3 2 1

For Diane, who never heard the good news; for Lucille, who got mixed messages; for Edwina, who still believes; for Patrice and Tom, who prepare the word; for those who told us their stories; and for all those still looking for "a faith to rouse them."

Contents

To the Reader

Jesus is too good to miss. That's the reason we've written this book, and chances are it's the reason you've picked it up. Life can be tough, mysterious, contradictory, and sometimes lonely. The idea that God has taken up with us, sharing the struggle and redeeming our suffering, makes life worth living. And it certainly makes dying a better proposition. If that faith lives in your heart, even in kernel form—or if you wish it did—you've come to the right place.

We'll put our cards on the table at the start. We're Catholics. And we're hoping to begin a conversation with those who once called themselves Catholic but are no longer sure that name applies. Obviously, if you're coming into this conversation, you have a lot of personal reasons for doing so. Maybe you left the Catholic Church behind, seemingly for good. Maybe you're still in the pews but finding it a struggle to stay there. You may be unsure of your faith and whether you even believe in God, let alone Jesus Christ or the Catholic Church. Perhaps you're eager to return but need only a nudge; or you may have been told that you weren't welcome. Maybe all you want right now is emotional or intellectual "sanctuary" to sort out your thoughts and feelings before you can decide whether you're in or out.

If being Catholic has been a problem for you, it may be a relief to know you're part of a big club. An estimated seventeen million baptized American Catholics are inactive, and two-thirds of all Catholics at some point in their lives interrupt their regular participation in the church. Those are big numbers, to be taken seriously. A church based on the reconciling and healing ministry of Jesus—with sacraments dedicated to our wholeness—has to provide a soft landing for those who have journeyed out and may be looking for a way back in. And because Jesus was always pretty gracious in his relationships with those who came to him from the highways and byways of life, it would also be helpful if the road back into the church could be traveled without judgment or shame. In fact, such a journey is cause for celebration on both sides. A friend who returned to the church after a twenty-year absence likes to shout across the auditorium before parish functions, "We are the church! We are the party!" She reminds us that Jesus wasn't kidding when he called his message good news, and good news is supposed to be a reason for joy.

But for a lot of Catholics—certainly for those who leave the church, even if only for a season—that sense of joy has been obscured. Before some of us can party, we have to be reminded what we're celebrating. That may mean tramping through some difficult territory first, and we hope this conversation will provide some companionship for entering that thorny terrain. If confusion, injury, anger, personal dilemmas, or other unresolved issues led you to leave the church or question your current participation in it, taking another look at those matters may provide healing for the past and hope for the future. If healing and hope are the results of this conversation, they alone are worth the price of admission! For those who decide to explore the possibility of reconciliation and reunion with the church, we'll also provide the information needed to begin that work.

Much of the trouble folks experience with the church, from within and from without, has to do with the authority of church teaching. That teaching is also paradoxically one of the first things Catholics and admirers name as among the great gifts the church has to offer. Certainly, one of the hallmarks of Catholic identity is the richness of an ancient church and its continuity of tradition. As Catholics, we are part of something bigger than ourselves, bigger than the present culture and the limited perspective of this generation. That larger sense of community across time and culture has a claim on us. But as the late Cardinal Joseph Bernardin once told his fellow bishops as quoted in a 1992 *Catholic Trends* article, "What we need now is to engage our people, to truly listen, to explain, to challenge, to show that our tradition really makes sense and, in the long run, better responds to their deepest longings and aspirations than anything else." Without this engagement and personal persuasion, we are left with the empty trappings of religion, hard to apply meaningfully to our lives and all too easy to leave behind.

On too many occasions, however, the tasks of engagement and persuasion were not even attempted. All that many of us seemed to hear was, "This is the church talking. Pray, pay, and obey." End of conversation. This is not only an abuse but even more sadly a tremendous waste of a precious, life-giving resource. What the Catholic tradition has to offer is a way for us to make sense of what is deepest in us. It gives us a meaningful framework for the relationships, events, and realities that mark our lives. We humans are caught between joy and suffering, the paradox of inhabiting a divinely inspired life bound by frustrating limitations and an expiration date. The church's purpose is to be the community that holds all of human experience together in one place with integrity, without cynicism or despair, and with confidence in the God who made us and awaits us along the horizon, where our finite vision falters.

Every great truth has its roots in a story, and the church's truths are no different. The kind of conversation we are proposing is a dialogue between your story, with all of its hard-won wisdom, and the story of the church. Each of us carries the "Scripture" of our life with us, complete with its saints and sinners, moments of revelation, and episodes of disintegration. The church's story begins with the Bible and continues through twenty-one centuries of divine revelation and sometimes all too human miscalculation. At the heart of the dialogue between our personal story and the great story of salvation history are the ever-present questions, Is there a place for me in the life of the church, and Is there a place in my life for the church? We'll try to provide you with the information and perspective you may need to answer that question thoughtfully, especially if you have been out of the pews for a while or feel you are not getting the answers you are looking for in your present parish. We'll provide some pegs to hang things on and some language to help you continue your reflection and choose your direction in peace.

It will come as no surprise to anyone reading this book that the church in the twenty-first century has its problems and that the church in every century has weathered its own storms. The following chapters will acknowledge those problems and the full humanity of an institution that, like the society around it, lives in conflicted and changing times, with old and new ways of thinking in apparent contradiction.

It is also no surprise that people feel compelled to step aside from participation in the life of the church for various reasons. Part of the responsibility we shoulder in these pages is to offer a medium for identifying the source of dissatisfaction, assessing the damage, and presenting possible avenues of repair. You're invited to reflect on what caused you to walk away in the first place or on why you're hanging on by your fingernails if you're still in the pews. The church experience may seem irrelevant to your faith. Mistreatment at the hands of church representatives in some critical hour may have soured you on the whole enchilada. The inability to reconcile what you believe—or don't believe—with what the church teaches may have caused your sense of communion to grind to a halt. Divorce and remarriage, gender and sexuality, issues surrounding the sanctity of life, and other fundamental considerations may have caused you to step away or to feel pushed. For some a simple, gradual drifting away and loss of connection that has no name and has never been closely examined may be at the root of the separation.

After examining what makes the Catholic experience stall for many, we'll pursue some of the reasons Catholics stay in the church or return to it. We'll explore how the life of the church in its fullness can name and give meaning to our everyday experiences, consecrating our relationships, achievements, failures, and lessons as holy ground. It is only through these experiences that we can meet the God who comes to us where we are.

In the end, we hope to assist in the clarification of what happens next. You may want more conversation or information; we'll point to resources you can consider. We'll also point out paths you can take to strengthen your spiritual journey. For those who want to work through some personal issues more deeply and formally, there are programs and processes for reconnecting to the church that have enabled many to make their way back. Others may prefer to slip back into the pews and pick up where they left off.

We have structured this book to move through a progression of considerations we hope will help distressed and distanced Catholics gain perspective on the church and their relationships to it. In chapter 1, we outline the problem of alienation in the church and define some of its effects on the alienated themselves, their families, and the community of the church as a whole.

Chapter 2 examines specific case histories of people who have left the church or feel no proper place within it. You may find your own voice echoed in their stories or, at the least, a link to the troubles—spiritual, emotional, and interpersonal—that occupy your present sense of dissatisfaction. As in any relationship, it is hard to get beyond the silence until it is established what this silence is about. What do you hear in the silence between you and the church? What went wrong, who is responsible, and what is the consequence of that failure?

Chapter 3 is a short course in "Theology 101." It outlines the basic principles of the religious quest in general and of the Judeo-Christian tradition in particular: Why go to church at all? How does belief in God lead us to a clearer understanding of the meaning of life? What does Christianity offer that would convince a person to embrace this faith and treasure it despite the adversities involved? In addition, chapter 3 includes a quick review of the story of salvation for those still unsure of how we got from the Bible to the church.

Chapters 4 and 5 pose two questions: (1) What do you want from the church? (2) What does the church want from you? (That is, what do you have to do to belong to the church—or belong to the church again?) These questions have to be asked separately because a dialogue has to have two free and distinct voices to achieve its purpose. These questions also require honesty and a bit of soul searching. If you have difficulty coming up with clear responses to the questions, it may be time to enlist an active listener, such as a spiritual director or friend willing to travel through these issues with you.

In chapter 6 we'll explore some criteria for finding a good and supportive parish for those considering reentry into the church or for those just seeking a port in a storm. Not all parishes are created equal, and sometimes what seems wrong with being Catholic is not universal but parish specific. There are "Camelots" out there—dream communities where membership is a joy and worship is life-sustaining. There are also "hellmouths," to borrow a phrase from *Buffy the Vampire Slayer*—places that seem particularly good at churning up conflict and experiences of the apocalyptic variety. Sometimes you can save yourself a lot of trouble by identifying and avoiding these toxic parishes. We'll suggest ways to find a parish that helps and doesn't harm your fragile truce with the church.

Chapter 7 will address those folks whose main problem with the church is spiritual hunger that has gone unmet. If your experience of being Catholic so far has seemed empty, shallow, boring, or unengaged, we'll offer some avenues for exploring a more vital connection.

In chapter 8 we'll listen to the voices of those who once left the church but chose to return as well as those who find a reason to stay despite their issues with the church.

For readers who are not convinced that the Catholic identity is viable for them, we include an epilogue that stands in for our blessing on the journey and our best wishes for peace.

We have also included a resources section, which lists print and online sources of information on Catholicism and alienated Catholics. In addition, the resources list some parish-based opportunities for beginning a conversation about your personal questions concerning your relationship to the church as well as Web sites that may help you pursue answers to those questions more actively. We recognize that for certain "unclubbable" or less extroverted personalities, this book stands in for the conversation, and we'll do our best to hold up our end here.

Being realistic, we recognize that for some, reconciliation with the church will be out of the question at this time or until hell (or the Vatican!) freezes over. For those who will take their leave of us at any point in this conversation, we hope you will take a blessing and the peace of Christ with you. God alone knows the contents of the human heart, and God's goodness and mercy have a long shelf life. If you've made it this far, you might as well see where the conversation goes from here. We appreciate the time you give us, and we'll work hard not to waste it.

Oh, by the way, as you move through these chapters, feel free to bring your sense of humor with you. Just because we're talking about God and religion doesn't mean it has to be grim. If you can get mad at or hurt by or disenchanted with the church, you can certainly afford to have a laugh or two, on the house. After all, if this *is* the church, then this *is* the party. So let the party begin.

ALICE L. CAMILLE
JOEL SCHORN

ONE

A Million Good Reasons to Leave

Driving home one evening, a friend learned we were interested in promoting a conversation with alienated Catholics. She stopped the car, looked over, and said, "You can talk to me."

She said this out of a depth of feeling, not without a tinge of anger and regret, doubt and longing, as if her experience with the church—and the fact that someone was interested in it—were still something deeply held, something that needed a good and living word spoken to it, whatever the final outcome. And she was quick to say she could put us in touch with a whole group of people we may want to talk with. The message has been the same almost everywhere we've gone; no researcher need go far to find someone who has left the church or is questioning the reasons he or she stays. We've all been to gatherings where the subject comes up, making a great conversation starter at cocktail parties or over dinner: What is *your* horror story about growing up Catholic? What happened to you while attending parochial school? The stories may be told with the intention to amuse or astonish or score the biggest grievance, but underneath it all, an unresolved injury or anger often remains.

But the wound may be deeper and closer to home. A family member stops going to church, quietly or dramatically, and it sets off a fireworks display between spouses or generations. From now on, every family gathering wears the shadow of this division. The subject, spoken or unspoken, hovers in the corners at each wedding and funeral, and every family crisis is inhabited by the anticipation of a scene. In the life of Catholics, there are hours when it is expected that the church will be engaged: marriages, births, rites of passage, serious illnesses, and death, at the barest minimum. Each time one of those delicate milestones is reached, the separation of family members from the church causes dissension at precisely the time we most need people to be pulling together. For families to be pulled apart in times of celebration or crisis is grievous. For the church to be the reason they are pulled apart is a contradiction tending toward the ludicrous.

The decision to leave the church is tough: on the individual who makes it, on the family who is pained or challenged by it, and less obviously but fundamentally, on the church itself, losing its members by way of the back door—along with all of their vitality, gifts, and purpose. A lot gets broken when a person makes such a choice, and too often the loss and damage are never healed or even addressed.

ALIENATION OF AFFECTION

There are a million reasons why people leave the church—or, more accurately, seventeen million reasons in this country alone, one for each person who currently relates to the term *ex, lapsed, former, nonpracticing, retired,* or, the hippest phrase, *recovering Catholic.* Of all the reasons we hear for this migration, nearly none could be described as frivolous, and many are quite poignant. The most common theme expressed among them all is a variation on the idea of "alienation of affection," a term used to contain the world of hurt involved in the death of a marriage. Once there was love, and good faith, and the potential for growth and a life together. But one side, or perhaps both parties, broke trust, and nothing has been done to reestablish what was lost.

According to Dean R. Hoge's landmark study *Converts, Dropouts, Returnees: A Study of Religious Change among Catholics* (New York: Pilgrim Press, 1981), around 40 percent of Catholics will waver in their commitment to the church at some point in their lives, for a season or longer. "Commitment" is generally defined by church attendance, although for some it may simply mean irregular or lukewarm involvement and for others no contact with the church at all. Of those underage who stop going to church or attend rarely, dissatisfaction with their Catholic identity is generally expressed when they have moved apart from their families and no longer feel obliged to attend. Conflict with the church's moral teachings, especially regarding sexual issues (premarital sex, birth control, abortion), is high on the list of reasons young adults drop out. Finally, a sense of irrelevance in the church experience—boredom at Mass, a disconnection between worship and "real life," or the inability to establish a clear link between Catholic practices and the message of the Bible—is a factor that leads the under-twenty-five crowd to loosen ties with the church.

Catholics over twenty-five who leave are conflicted in similar ways but with different precipitating factors. If they stop going to church because family pressure to attend wanes, it can be due to the loss of the more actively committed spouse or the end of the child-rearing phase of life. Older Catholics may object to church teachings, often in regard to divorce and gender roles as much as sexual or moral practices. They may feel their spiritual needs are not being served, because of changes in the church—or, at least as likely, because the church has not changed enough to keep up with the times. Those who leave the church later in life may cite the practice of confession, which they find to be fearful or objectionable. They are also likely to take responsibility for their departure by saying they are lazy or lack motivation to go to church. Though young adults most frequently exit when they leave home, older Catholics find the impetus for their departure in a conflict with a priest, moving to a new parish, divorce, or other significant life changes.

It is clear from Hoge's original study and his subsequent work on Catholics leaving and returning that dropping out almost invariably has to do with emotional and interpersonal issues. We are lead by our hearts as much as our heads in most matters, so it is no surprise that leaving the church is not an uncomplicated, rational process. Nor is it something we do in isolation from one another: those who leave the church frequently do so in response to changes in their relationships as a whole.

If relationships are a factor in our shifting membership in the church, then we have to consider the church itself as one element of the broader context of our relationships. After all, a satisfied and active member of the church is much less likely to depart from the pews when life changes occur and important relationships are on the ropes. Only the most intensely loyal Catholic would venture to argue that inadequacies in the church's local expression are not at fault in the departure of at least some of the seventeen million Catholics who separate from the church. Given Pope John Paul II's recent spate of apologies on behalf of the church—some one hundred were offered during the millennial Jubilee celebrations—it would seem that even the highest church authority is willing to take responsibility for a hundred reasons why people might leave the church. This is a good sign, and the appearance of multiple resources for former-and-potentially-future Catholics in some parishes is another sign that the church is beginning to accept a share of the blame for what has led to this state of alienation as well as to assume a role in the work of reconciliation. (More will be said about exploring reconciliation in chapter 5.)

Official recognition of a share in the blame is necessary if we, the active and the alienated Catholic together, are to move forward in this relationship. After the lengthening crisis of church leadership on public display in the early years of this new century, it will be harder to advance the argument of unquestioned obedience to the authority that has been so poorly used, as demonstrated in the sex abuse scandals. This loss of an unwieldy hammer is not to be regretted—and is perhaps the only outcome of the scandal not to be lamented. American Catholics will now expect and demand better reasons to follow their leaders than formerly submitted. "The church says so" will not be enough—if in fact it ever was.

Even those Catholics who do not consider leaving the church as an option often have serious issues with aspects of church teaching, practice, management, and vitality. As a result, those who remain active participants in the life of the church are not immune to feeling a touch of alienation now and then, from within the relationship—a coldness that any marriage partner will recognize and appreciate as part of the cycle of commitment. Traditional and progressive Catholics alike feel somewhat betrayed by the church when it changes, or doesn't change enough, in response to the times. Some women who exhibit a high level of involvement in their parishes still admit that they feel like second-class citizens within the church they love. Catholics who acknowledge a gay or lesbian orientation will readily speak of the spiritual schizophrenia it takes to claim membership in a community that officially calls their fundamental experience "gravely disordered." Folks who have never skipped a Sunday in their lives may admit that they go to church mostly out of habit or loyalty, not because of a soul-stirring encounter. When you start talking frankly with Catholics who are practicing their faith quite deliberately, you find that the choice to remain in the church cannot always be filed neatly under "Catholic with no issues to speak of."

But clearly, there is a distinction between Catholics with issues who stay nonetheless and those who depart. The distinction may be a matter of degree for some, but for others the breakup may seem more costly than remaining in a challenging but still meaningful relationship.

BREAKING UP IS HARD TO DO

James Joyce, in his novel *A Portrait of the Artist as a Young Man,* declared that there is no such thing as an ex-Catholic—only a lapsed one. He spoke with some experience, being an expatriate of Ireland who physically removed himself from his homeland and his church, only to spend the rest of his creative life writing about the identity he both loved and left behind. Not everyone who "used to be" Catholic feels haunted in this way. But many whose formal relationship with the church has been strained to the breaking point do speak of something unhealed or unwhole in moving apart from the community of faith that was once their home. Yet something has also malfunctioned in the relationship as they've experienced it so far, something that cannot be ignored. Though remaining active in the church may seem out of the question for some, denying the name Catholic may be equally troubling. As the rift widens for these seekers, so do the wound and the heartache. Whether such folks remain faintly in the pews or make their exit, something's missing. And that something has proved to be too important to do without.

For those born Catholic—that is, born into families that accepted the responsibility to baptize their children as infants—the relationship to the church may be in equal parts religious, ethnic, cultural, habitual, or simply inevitable. Cradle Catholics often have their earliest memories interwoven with experiences or expressions of faith—or at least of the religious trappings that go with it. Whatever was right or wrong in the first community of faith—the family—may become inextricably linked with our experience of church itself. Catholicism, in the universal sense, can only be as good as the Catholics we've known personally. It would be hard to be objective about an identity so intrinsic to the person who claims it. For example, if every lawyer we've ever known is a miserable, greedy cuss, how can we form an impression of lawyers in general that's any different? By contrast, if some lawyers we've met are the soul of integrity and generosity, whatever eventual opinion we form of the profession will have to grant that good lawyers exist.

Since the definition of *Catholic* is forged for so many of us in childhood, however, we may not have the luxury of waiting to meet the church in postadolescence to form an impression of what Catholicism "objectively" might be. The die is cast early, and the burden of proof weighs on the church to dispel or confirm our first and most intimate understanding of what it means to be a part of it. If we choose to leave the church as teens or in our young adulthood, it may be difficult for us to discern how much of what we're rejecting is Catholicism itself and how much of what we labeled "Catholic" is simply our parents' habitual and not always accurate expression of being Catholic. And the same factors that cause us to walk away may also keep us dragging the uneasy legacy behind us like Marley's chains in Dickens's *A Christmas Carol*. If our family is originally "the church" for us, then the church is also eerily inseparable from our family. It takes a real escape artist to slip out of that identity for good.

WHO GOES THERE?

The notion needs to be refuted at once: there is no "classic" former Catholic. No formula for alienating people is foolproof, as anyone who has ever tried to leave an aggressively romantic partner in the dust knows. It would be simplistic to assert that *A* leads to *B* and eventually to *E* for *Exit* in the matter of the church. In working with people on the other end of the spectrum—those who seek to join the Catholic Church as adults—it becomes apparent that people are unique all the way around the block, and certainly so in what they seek from religion. In the same way, what contributes to a sense of alienation in one person may be an attractive feature of church to another.

It must also be said that adults approach religious belief quite differently than children do, which can only be a good thing. Religion comes to children in the general context of what must be learned and incorporated, along with spelling, arithmetic, science, the names of distant relatives, and acceptable behavior. If a child's contact with religion is likewise an academic matter, as in parochial school or religious education programs, then the memorization of preestablished facts comes into play quite naturally. But by the time we emerge into the relative independence of adolescence, we are already insisting that the things we are asked to learn must also have some relevance for the experiences we are having. We are no longer content to incorporate "the facts" as enshrined in a textbook or in history; we also want them to be "true" in respect to the rest of what life is teaching us. By the time we reach adulthood, we approach religion with a fairly fixed set of questions we expect to have answered to our satisfaction based upon our life so far and its most significant issues. In other words, even for those of us who have never considered leaving the organized church of our youth, religion becomes in time a whole new ball game just the same. The church we once knew and were content to accept leaves *us,* in a sense, without our even being fully aware of its passing.

In the adult phase of religious query, then, questions must be asked and to some level of satisfaction addressed, if not answered entirely. What those questions are depends on the person, the personality, the life experience, and the church contact enjoyed or endured so far. When these issues are not addressed, not even voiced, rebuffed, answered negatively, or dismissed as unimportant or heretical, the person seeking answers will understandably make his or her way toward the door, mentally if not literally.

TAKING THE BLAME

If you are a disaffected Catholic, on any level, by any name, you may find a welcome validation in the description of why, how, and with what ramifications or burdens people choose to leave the church. There is supposed to be consolation in the kind of misery that has company, although that sort of company can backfire too. (Just think of your last family reunion or "support group" meeting.) Defining a situation is, at least, a helpful first step in determining how to proceed with it. But obviously it is not enough to describe a problem and then to shrug our shoulders about it. We have to take appropriate action to reach a place of greater resolution or harmony.

In choosing to initiate a conversation about the delicate matter of church disaffection, we recognize the thin ice all of us, writers and readers together, are skating on just to address this subject. It takes courage to engage the topic of hurt, anger, or disappointment from either side of a relationship, which is why we may choose to vent, mutter, or tell amusing stories about leaving the church but rarely speak heart to heart about it to someone who represents the other side—just as church officials have until recently avoided the issue of unhappy or disgruntled people formerly known as Catholic. Who wants to revisit the scene of the crime? Who wants to take the rap for whatever led to this division? Who wants to tramp back through all that gook?

In the interest of not passing the buck one more time, we hereby admit for the record, aloud and in print, that if you're mad or sad or disappointed with the Catholic Church, you probably have good reason to be. With a deep sigh, we admit that the church displays its share of mediocrity (or worse) in local celebrations of Mass and the sacraments and in preaching most of all. Those who come to the church looking for spiritual nourishment or moral guidance have sometimes been simply bored to tears by an indifferent and passionless ritual. Some of what passes for religious instruction may also be badly led, poorly explained, or barely funded. Adult religious education is often nonexistent. Certain demographics, like teens or single adults or people of color, are regularly ignored, especially where staffs are small and money is tight. The quality of spiritual and moral leadership may be lacking or uneven from one diocese to another.

We ourselves have felt that members of the church hierarchy sometimes challenge our intelligence, not to mention our adulthood, in their presentation of the role of the laity. We've also seen how church representatives have, at times, distorted the Christian message for less than Christian purposes, such as in the interests of maintaining control. When the church speaks of "unity," sometimes it really means uniformity, demanding submission to its teachings without any "but's." To preserve itself as an institution, maintain its own authority, or shield itself and its leaders, the church has sometimes acted suspiciously like the religious leaders Jesus condemned in his own generation. Officials of the church, historically and with some regularity, have been willing to sacrifice people in order to preserve their own sense of tradition—even at the expense of what would later be acknowledged by the church itself as "truth." The church's treatment of Joan of Arc and Galileo and its historical record on abolition and anti-Semitism are a few examples. And all this has happened too often, on and off, for nearly two thousand years. That's a lot to forgive, and the fact that no one may be asking for forgiveness doesn't make it any easier.

In short, like many who may see themselves in the refuse pile of church membership, we admit that as card-carrying Roman Catholics we have experienced the push to the margins from the church we love and remain active within. We have seen how the mechanism of the church can get in the way of the message it is supposed to announce to the world, sometimes by acting as if the church itself were the message. The church runs into trouble when it obscures the gospel—by talking too much about itself and not enough about the good news of Jesus. Considering the fact that the church came into existence to proclaim the gospel and continue the presence of Christ on earth, this is a serious flaw. The institution of the church, like all of its members, is quite human and, as such, is in need of a full and honest confession of its failings from time to time, not to mention the required contrition and resolution to avoid these sins in the future with the help of God's grace.

BLAMING THE MESSENGER

Of course, institutions are by nature power conglomerates, established for the purpose of preserving and passing on their goods to their membership. That's what institutions are for and do best, and the church is no exception. For twenty centuries organized Christianity has preserved and passed on the gospel—the good news of Jesus Christ—the creed of the apostles, the gift of the sacraments, and the wisdom of our forebears. But the same power structures at work to preserve a legacy can be equally rigid about maintaining it in status quo. Institutions rarely bow or bend, much less acknowledge fault or admit the need for change.

So when an institution's members agitate for change or challenge any aspect of the tradition, the agitator may well end up bearing the blame. This time-honored practice is known as scapegoating. As it originally worked, the people of a society accumulated a problematic amount of wrongdoing that had to be reconciled with the heavens at the highest cost: life itself. Rare cultures resorted to human sacrifice, appeasing the gods with the blood of a favored person, such as a firstborn son or virgin daughter. More civilized societies employed the scapegoat, who symbolically carried the sins of the people out of town. The scapegoat was driven into the wilderness or off a cliff, taking the guilt of the populace with it. It's a nice solution, for everyone but the goat.

The goats are safe these days, but those who raise the voice of dissent (in church, as in government or elsewhere) may find themselves saddled with guilt and ushered out of town quite hastily. Theologians who question the company line of tradition with their scholarship may be silenced or removed from positions in the official centers of church teaching. Bishops who speak with a prophetic edge might find themselves permanently assigned to govern over the Mojave Desert. Pastors who do not keep pace—fast or slow—with the rest of their deanery of priests may not only become friendless but be removed to a corner of the diocese where they can do the least "damage" with their out-of-step ideas. Laypeople who are too "uppity" may be marginalized within the assembly to the point of de facto censure. Those who want a more moderate or traditional approach to change are as likely to be shuttled aside as those who pursue a more radical future for the church. And of course, for those who are deemed really problematic, there's always excommunication, rarely used but incisively effective.

But blaming the messenger isn't just a threat from the official level of the church. The blame game that counts for most of us is much more intimate. The spouse who quits going to church because the priest is a bigot or because the message is always about money can find himself or herself being treated like a moral pariah by the churchgoing partner for rejecting what is objectionable. So too parents are tempted to harass their grown children about church attendance when their offspring might have specific and identifiable grievances with the church that are given no hearing. Even those who choose to remain in the pews but ask critical questions about church practices could find themselves viewed not as the canary in the mines that warns of a nonviable atmosphere but as a wolf in the fold that must be eliminated or subdued.

And if your first marriage failed and a second marriage is deemed irregular according to church standards, or your sense of alienation from the modern Mass makes you feel abandoned by the church you grew up with, somehow that too becomes your problem in the assessment of blame and responsibility. If you can't find your way past your dispiriting parochial school experiences or the dysfunctional father who terrorized you about Catholic moral principles that were somewhat idiosyncratic to say the least, that becomes your fault and part of the burden you carry.

Any way you look at it, being dissatisfied with your present experience of the church is tough enough; being blamed as the source of the problem is a double whammy. Of course, no one ever said that speaking the truth would bring you love and acceptance. None of the biblical prophets received a polite reception when bringing their complaint to the authorities, and some of them were beaten, imprisoned, exiled, or murdered for delivering their critique. In the "misery loves company" category, a religious dissenter may enjoy a fine society indeed.

WHERE DO WE GO FROM HERE?

We have taken some time in this chapter to consider the position of alienated Catholics in general and the reasons practicing church members may find themselves distanced from the community emotionally or demographically. We've also spent some time looking at the trouble, both personal and contextual, this alienation causes for those who separate from the assembly and the faith of their families. It would be insensitive to rush past the source of the strife without expressing the legitimacy, gravity, and complexity of the conflict or without mourning the pain that results for many who feel the loss of a fundamental element of their identity. Home is where the heart is; our hearts are nowhere as deeply attached as in the relationship between us and our Maker. When we are alienated from the church, it can feel like being abandoned by our family of origin or running away from home, depending on the direction of the break. Even when we have good reasons for being on the outs with the church, many still find there is unfinished business or unhealed wounds to attend to. Still others may hold hopes for a dialogue that never took place, for the possibility of somehow working things out or at least declaring a truce, for one last chance to turn the sword into a plowshare. For those who drifted away from a superficial experience of faith that never developed roots, the lingering sentiment of having missed something crucial may still need to be addressed.

The next chapter examines specific case histories of people who have left the church or feel they can find no proper place within it. You may find your own voice echoed in their stories or, at the least, discover in them a link to the troubles—spiritual, emotional, or interpersonal—that occupy your present sense of dissatisfaction. As in any relationship, it is hard to get beyond the silence until it is established what the silence is about. What do you hear in the silence between you and the church? What went wrong, who is responsible, and what is the consequence of that failure? And what, if anything, should be done about it?

TWO

Examining the Root Cause of Departure

The question posed by earlier generations was, How could someone leave the church? For Catholics raised before the Second Vatican Council of the 1960s, that choice was mystifying and troubling. But for many baptized baby boomers and their children, the question is now often framed in the reverse: Why would someone choose to *remain* in the church? The onus of responsibility has shifted, in recent times, from making the case for departure to confirming the reason for participation. This is not simply a Catholic phenomenon but can be seen society-wide in response to social obligation and commitment. Of course, the right to dissent has always been a fundamental American option, and it could be said that U.S. Catholics are just catching up to the rest of the culture when they exercise freedom of speech and opinion in the particular sphere of their religion. Since the massive movement to question authority culminated in the 1960s, with the Vietnam War, civil rights, sexual mores, and gender roles coming under critical review all at once, the implicit trust once invested in institutions to make up our minds for us seems to have been reexamined across the board. It is almost quaint to observe from the perspective of the twenty-first century that we no longer give knee-jerk allegiance to what the government, the church, the press, the experts, or our parents say. It is difficult to imagine that fifty years ago these authorities were less frequently called into question, at least aloud. Now that the culture has moved in another direction, it would be hard to put that particular genie back in the bottle.

At least part of the reason that leaving the church overtly (as opposed to checking out mentally) became more common after the 1960s is that it became more culturally acceptable to make such a choice. Of the current millions of "expatriate" Catholics in the United States alone, one might imagine that the majority of them would have stayed put in an earlier generation, fuming under their breath or nursing a passive aggression about the whole matter of religious participation. Older folks may recall the group of men who used to sit in their cars or smoke on the church steps while their wives "heard" Mass or the numbers of women and men who stood in the back or jostled for the last pew, hoping for a mercifully quick escape at the earliest opportunity. Today these marginal adherents would likely feel freer just to stay home altogether or perhaps to find a more compatible religious environment.

If our heightened sense of freedom coupled with a deepening suspicion of authority has made it easier to walk away from church attendance in the past few decades, the reasons we might do so have not changed significantly. For many Catholics who stop participating in the life of the church at some level, then as now, the separation grows out of a disconnection between their own lives— daily experience accumulated over years—and what the church has offered them.

For the purposes of this discussion, it seems useful to consider the issues that separate Catholics from their church in the general categories of faith, institution, and community. Obviously, these three elements of religious life cannot be perfectly distinguished, and many of their features overlap. But for the sake of surveying the terrain of distress and dissent, these categories are broad enough to establish some grounds for the conversation. To understand how these three issues come between us and our place in the church, we have only to listen to those who are struggling to stay or who have already gone.

FAITH: WHEN BELIEF IS THE ISSUE

At first glance, the religious notion of faith appears to be a relatively simple thing. For some people belief in the existence of God brings everything into focus in a way that makes sense. For others faith in a deity is just not rational or, as far as they can see, possible. There can be thousands of shades and gradations of doubt in between, but most people find themselves basically in agreement with or in denial of the existence of a higher power of some sort. This causes conflict when people whose lives are intimately entwined find themselves on either side of the faith divide.

"I don't believe in God, and neither does Cathy," Robert said in a quiet voice as he addressed his prospective father-in-law. "So there won't be a church wedding." This short statement dropped into the silence like a bombshell, and the parents could be seen holding in their breath. Three things they hadn't expected on that Sunday afternoon had just shown up uninvited in their living room: An atheist was marrying their daughter! Their daughter had been revealed as a nonbeliever! Their marriage would not be witnessed by the church! For this Catholic family it was the end of the world as they had known it.

But the young couple did not back down from their decision. As they saw it, the churchgoing folks they knew were mostly hypocrites. People went to Mass on Sunday and then lived out the rest of the week in a completely independent world of values and priorities. Cathy admitted she had stopped believing when she was twelve years old. Jesus seemed like a heroic enough figure, but no one was able to prove that he wasn't more than a fairy tale or literary character. His death was awful and meaningless, and the stories of the saints and martyrs that followed were mostly used as scare tactics to keep children in line. If all of this were real, and so important, Cathy reasoned, wouldn't the whole world be different than it is?

And so Cathy and Robert, raised Catholic, were married by the justice of the peace. And they chose not to baptize the children that came later. The hurt between the generations remained unresolved.

A crisis of faith is bound to cause a breach in a person's relationship with the church. If you've lost faith in the existence of God, the church as a community of faith is rendered pointless. If science or human reason is enough to answer all of your questions about the world around you, religion becomes irrelevant, and Christianity or Catholicism is beside the point.

This kind of pure atheism may be uncommon, or, at most, periodic and circumstantial within a given personal history. They say there are no atheists in foxholes, and some who doubt religious answers all their lives may begin to doubt their doubts in times of crisis or serious illness. After twenty-five years of good and loving marriage, Robert and Cathy faced a terrible challenge. Cathy was taken ill with cancer. In her last year she asked several of her family members to explain again why they believed in God and what they thought waited beyond death. On the hospital admission form, she wrote "Catholic" in the box marked "Religious Preference." She accepted a visit from the chaplain and asked him many questions, though she appeared dissatisfied with his answers. She did not choose to receive last rites. But it's clear that Cathy was still reaching out for something worthy of her hopes, in which to put her faith when she died.

Does the church have anything to offer someone who rejects the basic tenet of belief in the divine? Certainly, the response of the Catholic family to the announcement of disbelief is the primary witness the church offers. A sympathetic and loving response will leave a door open for reconsideration in the future. An angry and accusing reaction will make reconciliation at a later date less likely. Every contact with the believing family becomes equated with the testimony of the church, as do future encounters with Catholics in general, up to the chaplain's final visit in the hospital. None of these interactions will necessarily lead a person to the perspective of faith, but they can most certainly cement the wall against it if they are negative experiences.

FAITH: WHEN RELIGIOUS UNDERSTANDING IS THE ISSUE

Theology can be a dirty word for those who equate it with dry, academic chatter about Being and Essence. But theology is really only the description of the God you believe in. Sometimes the thing that pulls people out of the pews is not doubt in the existence of God but rather the sense that the God they believe in is different from the one they are hearing about in church. Their inherent theology, or understanding of God, is leading them elsewhere.

If you have a faith crisis that is basically theological, it can take many forms. It could be that what the Catholic Church teaches is not what you believe or that it no longer reflects what you can put your faith in because of your personal life experience so far. But often it is really the *presentation* of the church's faith that is at fault; that is, you might find harmony with the church's teaching about God, but all you get on Sunday is Father Ed's ongoing diatribe about God's wrath against sinners. Or perhaps you would find yourself in absolute communion with the teaching of the church if only you could hear it for what it actually is, beyond the media distortions and what Sister Rita explained to you in the seventh grade—neither of which is entirely accurate.

For Ernesto it was obvious that the Catholic moral system demonstrated to him didn't jibe with the world he was living in. In the Bible, Jesus talked about charity, justice, and compassion. His first-generation American family didn't have much use for those ideas! They practiced Old World punishment—"spare the rod and spoil the child"—and the God they believed in nodded his consent from heaven. When Ernesto grew up, moved away, and attended Mass in other cities, he kept listening for a preacher who was going to talk about the Jesus who he felt sure was represented in the Gospels. But no dice: Ernesto met that tough-guy God everywhere he went. He kept reading the Bible at home for confirmation that he wasn't crazy, that his Jesus really existed. Finally, a coworker told him about a Lutheran church across town that had a lively sense of worship and a welcoming community. Ernesto attended one Sunday and never looked back. Here, at last, was the Jesus he was looking for!

Often Catholics who leave the church because of faith issues don't exit Christianity outright. They don't object to religion, even in its organized form, and they may be quite spiritually committed. If you are unable to match your inner conviction with the faith of the church as it's presented to you, it is not surprising that another Christian church or even another religious tradition that does so may be appealing. Some folks may also abandon organized religion completely to follow a more personal path that is explicitly "spiritual" or perhaps simply a way of pursuing truth on whatever terms the truth may come.

Ernesto is often characterized by his family members as a heretic, or "fallen away" in his faith, or lacking in some way. Actually his faith life is of great interest to him, and he is dedicated to living it with integrity and to raising his daughter as a Christian. He expresses regret that he couldn't find this kind of community within Catholicism ("It would have been a lot easier for everyone concerned," he admits), but he is grateful for the faith community he now enjoys, which supports him in the way of Christian discipleship.

Of course, a practicing Catholic wants to point out that such positive expressions of the Christian message *are* available within Ernesto's original faith tradition, even if one must admit that the other kind of parishes exist too. But the good Catholic parish quite simply wasn't there for Ernesto. His conscience led him to seek and find the face of God as he understood it, and in his case the Lutherans beat the Catholics to the punch. If that faithful expression of the gospel didn't happen in a Catholic context in Ernesto's experience, whose fault is that? The Catholicism "on the books" is not as real or compelling, for most of us, as the Catholicism we encounter in Catholics.

INSTITUTION: PROBLEMS ON SUNDAY MORNING

Nancy is not ready to leave the church, just yet. But she talks about how Mass attendance "has become a boring chore." She and her husband go, she says, "because it's the right thing to do, but not because we have that urge to go. If we find it boring, I can completely understand why the younger parishioners don't want to go either. We feel the church has not kept up with the times, but at the same time some rules that should have been kept are being ignored."

Nancy's situation is not uncommon. But it could be more a problem with the local style of religious expression, or even the present pastoral leadership, than it is a fundamental problem with Catholicism. Some parishes are strapped for cash and can't afford a state-of-the-art music ministry. And not all priests are created equal, with a gift of eloquent, moving, and original preaching. Even where both of these factors collide, the worship experience can still be redeemed if the pastor is humble or creative enough to encourage lay collaboration and participation in the work of public worship.

But where the lack of strong, gifted leadership proves to be an insurmountable obstacle, sometimes finding another parish community is the answer. In large urban communities there may be a dozen Catholic churches within driving distance, each serving as a "magnet" parish for a specific group: families with children, the college community, or people who hunger for the more traditional style. You may even be able to attend a Latin Mass at the monastery just out of town. Maybe a short drive away, Nancy and her husband would be sitting up straight in the pew, amazed at the vitality of an engaged assembly or challenged by an outreach-oriented parish that calls them to a heightened awareness of their responsibility to the greater community around them.

On the other hand—maybe not. If they happen to live in a rural area or a particularly sluggish and incompatible diocese, there may not be another Catholic parish within fifty miles. Or the parishes out there may be worse than the one they already attend. But church-shopping may not be the answer to their dilemma at all. Attending an evening of reflection about the meaning of Catholic rituals like the Mass might deepen their appreciation of the Sunday morning experience. Joining a parish-sponsored Bible study or prayer group to augment their sense of belonging to the community might make Sundays feel more involving. And if such groups or adult enrichment opportunities don't exist, Nancy and her husband might find their place in the parish by beating the bushes and starting one themselves.

Another woman, Renee, also finds herself bored at Mass. But other Catholic moments give her the opposite experience: "Confession is stressful." She misses the Latin Mass: "Even though I didn't understand the words, it added to the spirituality and mystery of Christ being there in the tabernacle." Renee struggles with the loss of a traditional style of Catholic worship, but at the same time she'd like to see a modernizing of other aspects of church. "Maybe," Renee says, "if the church joined the real world and admitted its own mistakes, allowed priests to marry, gave equality to women, and recognized that for people who make bad judgments in their lives, there is forgiveness," she might be more comfortable in the pews.

It is not unusual for people to "want it both ways" like Renee— to hunger for some aspects of the "old" church and still expect the inclusion of today's or tomorrow's ideas in it. A lot of us have ambivalent or inconsistent attitudes about change: we recognize it's inevitable and yet we'd like to have it on our own terms. A custom-made church might require smaller parking lots (like some Protestant churches that are offshoots of offshoots); in some cases, it might indeed be easier to stay parked in your own garage if your designer church is really one-size-fits-me. But maybe "easy" isn't the best route to take in the spiritual life; taking the path of least resistance might actually be self-defeating. The business of church implies other people; in fact, that's the best reason to join a church—to commit to the communal work of mutual support and challenge.

For Renee making time for regular retreats in a monastic setting might satisfy her desire for sacred space and traditional prayer, while still supplying the element of community. She might even discover a vocation within her that is seeking expression, or at least a vital connection to the often very progressive spirit of some monastic communities that would free her from the sense of hitting a gendered glass ceiling in parish life. Who knows, but that "church in the real world" she is looking for may become redefined in the process.

Jim left the Catholic Church because the repetitiveness of the services turned him off. "The overstructured Mass services," he says, "didn't make me feel like I was giving the true honor that God deserves." He decided he needed to choose for himself a way of worship in which his "participation is from within, not from following the pack." While he doesn't think the church should do anything to make it easier for him to participate, he also believes some of its "traditions and ceremonies are too structured and have lost some meaning over the centuries."

Jim doesn't seem to be asking for much, and he's certainly moving in a direction different from that of someone like Renee. Actually he's asking for *less* than he's getting. Less formula, less pomp and circumstance. Less of the same old thing, which, for Jim, is predictable to the point of being deadening. Maybe he'd find what he is looking for in another Catholic setting, but the problem for him could be organized religion as a whole. Some people will never be comfortable in a ritual situation, always feeling it chafe like a shirt with a stiff collar. Some fidgety types will endure the liturgical setting for the sake of other benefits they see in being Catholic: Christian faith, access to the sacraments, moral teaching, a sense of joining together for a common and meaningful purpose. They may never be really comfortable inside the "straitjacket" of ritual worship, but they appreciate other aspects of their faith tradition enough to put up with the discomfort. Yet others who have not developed that additional sense of connectedness may simply bolt when the worship style gets to be too much for their personality type. Folks like Jim sometimes get lucky, finding a parish where the priest is no more comfortable with exacting ritual than he is. Such a priest may adopt a very loose and informal way of celebrating the Mass that would make Jim sigh with relief and sink into the nearest beanbag chair.

"I used to be a Mass junkie," Margo declares. "I signed up to be a reader or to give out communion every weekend. Sometimes I went to Mass five times on a holy day because I always had some role to perform. And I belonged to every parish committee there was. I hung out at the church more than the *priests.*" Margo has not been to church for two years now. The reason: a change of leadership in the parish. To Margo, being Catholic was defined by the former pastor's style of running a parish and leading the assembly in worship. Once the "new guy" showed up, however, she didn't recognize what became of the parish she was devoted to. The original pastor was a terrific and lively preacher. The new guy was not very gifted; his halting homilies never seemed to go anywhere. The pastor she loved let her run the liturgy and finance committees, while the new priest was much more protective about "his turf."

"Father Steve didn't mind that I was 'Mrs. Pastor,' and he let me be in charge and appreciated my help," Margo says ruefully. "But Father Dan is afraid of me and doesn't want me to have too much power. So he limited what I can do, to the point where I don't even want to be there."

Margo's problem is complex because she has probably been poorly served by both pastors. Collaborative ministry between clergy and laity remains a tightrope walk, and allowing one parishioner so much authority can dampen the response of others who may be equally prepared to be leaders. As pastors are reassigned, the new priest may be less comfortable with the hands-off approach preferred by the old one or may feel aced out by a team that did not form naturally out of his own administrative style. The conflict may lie simply in a misunderstanding or lack of communication. But it could also be that Margo's real problem is that her identity as a Catholic is wrapped around a perceived role and not around a core belief in what her baptism offers her. She may equate being Catholic with doing things in and around the parish. Margo's time away from the church may be an opportunity for her to consider what it really means to her to be Catholic.

INSTITUTION: PROBLEMS WITH CHURCH TEACHING

"The church seems more and more focused on the maintenance of its worn traditions and power structures, as well as less and less responsive to lay Catholics," Diane says. "It is embedded in an out-dated governmental structure, and it is blind to its injustice to women and other groups. By remaining in the far past—for example, by rationalizing its exclusion of women from positions of authority and power—it risks alienating large segments of the American membership. The church seems addicted to power, but Jesus' message negated the traditional human reliance on power."

Diane has a point—actually several points—to make in her inability to put up with membership in the Catholic Church much longer. She's an educated person, successful and well regarded in her professional life and treated with basic respect in every corner of her life. Except by the church. The dissonance is starting to make her wonder if she's going nuts every time she steps inside that building on Sunday. But the idea of stepping outside of her Catholic identity and being forced to hit the road, spiritually speaking, makes her angry. Why should she have to leave? This is her home, and she has a right to be here! But sometimes this feels like the only right the church affords her.

Other people wonder about the barriers the church seems to put up between people and God. "Sometimes," Karen says, "I get the feeling that the pope, the cardinals, even priests get more attention than God does. I feel sometimes like the church has put all of these layers between the people and God. I question who the church has as its authority—God or the pope." Sharon's thoughts are similar: "I can have a personal relationship with God without having to show up at a certain place at a certain time once a week and recite from memory words that have very little meaning for me. I also don't like how that one man, the pope, is (practically) revered as some deity on earth when in reality he's just a man with ailments and fears and faults like anyone else."

The question of church structure and hierarchy, as these women describe it, is a stumbling block for many accustomed to living in a more democratic arrangement with power. Why aren't women included in positions of authority in the church? Why are all these layers of hierarchy necessary to begin with? What is our proper relationship to "that one man" who seems to be running the whole show for the one billion members of the church worldwide? This is not simply a problem for female Catholics; many men in the church, some of them ordained, ask themselves similar questions and are troubled by the available answers. Monsignor Al laments that he is sometimes torn between his responsibility to faithfully represent the church that gives him authority to teach and the voice of his conscience, which occasionally moves him, after thirty years of pastoral ministry, to arrive at other conclusions. "I believe in the God who speaks to me in Scripture, the sacraments, and the tradition of the church," he says. "But I hear God speak in the lived reality of the people I know and love, who are also the church. How can I choose to hear one voice and not the other?"

Issues surrounding the authority of the church are closely linked to problems with church teaching, since both come from the same source, known as the church magisterium, or teaching authority. The church claims this teaching authority as its apostolic mandate (that is, its mandate from the apostles). Michael expresses a conflict with the magisterium when he says that, according to his perception, "church teaching is all about sex: contraception, abortion, fear of women, celibacy, what have you." Joe experiences the conflict and frustration from another perspective: "I love the church with all my heart and soul—but it's murdering me too. They can't accept me gay, and I can't go there and play it straight."

Of course, for every person who feels the church is living in the past when it comes to certain of its teachings, there is another who wishes the church would return to the more trusted world of a generation or two ago, with its perceived greater dignity and purity of moral principles. "The church has become indistinguishable from the culture," Amanda says with disgust. She is a young Catholic, not old enough to remember the way things were as her mother and grandmother describe them. "I go to confession, and the priest tells me my sins are not sins but only part of coming to maturity as a person. What is all this psychological junk? I want the church to tell me what's right and wrong!"

Chris, in his fifties, couldn't agree more: "These days, you go to one priest, and he'll let you off. You go to another, and he'll throw the book at you. Church teaching is relative now, all about not trying to offend anyone. I hate this politically correct stuff!"

Moral relativism is not and has never been an official church position. Rather the magisterium seeks a balance between establishing moral principles and practicing a softer pastoral engagement with individuals caught in the matrix of their own personal stories and circumstances. This is popularly known as "distinguishing between the sinner and the sin." Church teaching, for example, judges the termination of an unborn life to be morally wrong, but the woman struggling within the context of a crisis-inducing pregnancy ought to receive a response from the church that expresses the full compassion of Christ, even if she chooses to have an abortion. Anything less than this may sound like a strictly valid use of church authority, but by Gospel standards it is unjustifiable.

For those who find themselves on the oppressed or excluded end of church teaching, there are decisions to be made. Sometimes a further examination of church teaching—such as reading a book on moral theology or taking a class sponsored by the diocese on the teachings of Vatican II—may provide a wider and more sympathetic understanding of the church's positions. At times this understanding may even lead to a change in one's personal position or a reconciliation of the conflict. But it may also confirm that, for you, the choices you are making are the right ones. If you are at odds with the church on something important to you, consider that you may be called to be a prophetic voice within the church on this issue. The commitment to being a community of faith includes the responsibility to remain in dialogue and to grow in understanding together.

COMMUNITY: THE CHURCH IS THE RELATIONSHIP

The church is more than just a deposit of teachings about the faith and more than a governing institution that dictates behavior. It is also, by definition, our relationship to the Body of Christ as we experience our union with God and one another. But how real is that union, and how well does the church mirror that relationship in its treatment of its members?

Therese, who is African American, attended a largely white and Hispanic city parish. She says, "I felt unwelcome even though I went for several years. Many of the elderly parishioners seemed unwilling to shake my hand during the sign of peace at Mass. No part of my heritage was acknowledged. After several years of feeling uncomfortable and unwelcome, I stopped attending Mass."

Once upon a time in this country, Catholic communities were deliberately geared to welcome the stranger, since the memory of being a stranger was acute in the immigrant population. Parishes developed a particular ethnic character and mission: for Poles, Italians, Germans, Irish. Then the "melting pot" ideal took effect, and differences were presumably blended away. These days, in some of these same parish communities, there is resistance to making room on the roster for a Mass in Spanish, Tagalog, or Vietnamese. African Americans report an ongoing sense of exclusion and omission in the church that feels remarkably like racism. When no distinctly "Black Catholic" parish is available, they may feel marginalized, invisible, or downright snubbed in a white or mixed parish.

Sometimes only a single slight can drive someone away for years, even a lifetime. Karen remembers clearly the day she left the church. She had been very involved in the church and was content within her circle of Catholic friends. Then she made friends with some people who were not Catholic and who had some challenging questions for her about her faith. She didn't have answers, but she wanted them; so she went to a priest for help. Unfortunately, he did not have time for her, gave her a business card, and told her to call him back in a couple of weeks.

It may seem a small thing—a priest being too busy at the time to help a young person experiencing doubts—but church occupies sacred space for most of us, and lots of energy gets released when that ideal is violated. Quite simply, we expect more from the

church than we do from the secular world. When church person-
nel demonstrate that they're only human, it can feel like a betrayal.
To lose faith in the ideal of church can seem like losing faith in
God. For many the difference between the two is not always clear.
The story is quite common: an insensitive remark from a representative of the church during a wedding or a funeral, an offensive
homily, even telling an altar boy to get a haircut, can be devastating to people who are strongly bound to the church and whose
emotional bond makes them all the more vulnerable to being hurt
in that context. As Therese observes, "I never joined another
church or switched to another denomination because I always
considered myself Catholic. I continued to have a relationship
with God which wasn't affected by which parish I attended. I simply didn't go to Mass anymore." Some might judge the faith of
such people as weak or poorly placed, contending that a vital faith
would be able to withstand the occasional slight or insult from a
thoughtless individual. But moments of devastation also register
the strong desire of Catholics to put faith in the church, to be part
of it, and to offer their service within it.

Of course, it doesn't take a deliberate act of commission, like
racism, or omission, like the absence of a caring exchange, to
encourage the feeling of alienation. Some folks simply do not
experience the parish as a welcoming place, period. It's a filling
station for the sacraments, a place to drop your money in the basket, and an obligation to be met on holy days. "Nobody would
notice if I was there or not," Brian says with a hint of reproach.
"Why should I go? The ushers barely look at you when you say
hello, and the people who read the readings and give out communion belong to their special clique. The rest of us have no real
function. People don't talk to each other, and all the talk about
community is phony. Last time I was there, the woman in the pew

glared at me when I asked her to move in so I could sit down. What kind of community is that?"

Brian is right; that's no kind of community, and his experience is unfortunately not unique. For Catholics raised in parishes that took the silence-is-golden approach to worship, talking in church or even making eye contact with another person is considered irreverent. Such folks—along with others who for their own reasons simply aren't friendly—view their time in church as between them and God, and that leaves the idea of neighbor out of the loop. This has led to a clash of cultures between those who are seeking a vital experience of community in parish life and those who, like Greta Garbo, "vant to be alone." Sometimes parish leadership in steering the assembly around to a warmer or more tolerant way of behaving would ease the tension between the two groups. But often the only solution is to have the 7:00 AM "quiet Mass" followed by the hand-gripping, family-friendly liturgy at 9:00. Perhaps if Brian changed his attendance to another Mass in the same parish, he'd find a heartier reception.

Therese, Karen, and Brian expressed reasonable expectations of their church, yet they were hurt and disappointed with the response they received. Sometimes the hurt comes at a very critical time in a person's life, in circumstances that even the most thoughtless church leader ought to think twice before stumbling on—it can be delicate territory where even angels fear to tread. Anne had had two miscarriages already, so when her third baby was born dead, the anguish was incomprehensible. She called the parish, asking if a priest could come out to baptize the child. The response she got can hardly be believed: "The church doesn't baptize the dead." Needless to say, what the priest said is technically correct, but pastorally speaking, nothing could be more wrong. The death of a child is no time for a lesson in church law. What Anne needed more than anything was a consoling, faithful presence. What she got was callous legalism. She never set foot in a church again. Even her Catholic family members did not question her choice.

COMMUNITY: LIFE CHANGES AND CHALLENGES

There's nothing easy about facing the end of a marriage. The loss of a partner, the impact on children, the potential for economic instability, and the death of love are all sad and fearful aspects of divorce. All of that is bad enough; but when rejection is felt from the church as well, it adds insult to injury. Divorce and remarriage are two fragile moments when a Catholic's bond to the church can break. Sometimes it's just a matter of having received inaccurate information or bad advice: divorced Catholics often were told or simply believe that the church prohibits them from participating in the sacraments. Catholics who remarry outside the church may likewise be unaware of options the church offers to annul their previous marriage and recognize a new one. Those who do know of these options may have met resistance or ineptitude from church officials, or they may think the solution offered to them is long, humiliating, unnecessary, difficult, or expensive. And for reasons quite apart from marital issues, some Catholics believe themselves to be "excommunicated," or outside of the church, because of something they have done. They have no idea how to gain the information or pastoral advice they need to dispel that assumption or to return to practicing their faith with assurance and a sense of welcome. (See chapters 6 and 7 for more about how to get good pastoral advice.)

As a young woman, Lucille fell in love with a man who was a Mormon. She didn't know the first thing about the Mormon Church, but reflexively she sought advice from her parish priest about it. He told her bluntly that if she married a Mormon, she was barred from communion and the sacraments. This thought was scary to Lucille, but she was young and in love. Love ruled the day, and she married the fellow. Considering herself effectively excommunicated, she joined the Mormon Church to be closer to her husband. Though the marriage failed in the upcoming years, Lucille remained in the Mormon Church and married her second husband from within that community. "It never occurred to me to go 'home' to Catholicism," she says frankly. "They told me I was out, and there was no home to return to." The fact that her Catholic parents were horrified by her marriage outside of the church and wanted little to do with it confirmed for her that being Mormon was better than remaining "a Catholic in bad standing." The Mormons offered her a sense of belonging that she could count on.

Sometimes Catholics can lose connection with the church as a result of more mundane life changes. Children grow up and move away. Siblings scatter to different parts of the country. Job changes and educational opportunities require people to move every few years. Our highly mobile society makes it difficult for people to establish continuity in their lives, and each move interrupts the process of establishing and maintaining connections to a church. Often people move and can't find a welcoming and satisfying parish in the next city. Children, who are dragged along with each successive move, may miss the opportunity to celebrate the sacraments of first communion or confirmation along with their age group if they don't arrive in time to fulfill the sometimes staggering requirements of parish prep programs. As adults, missing out on the fullness of membership guaranteed by their baptism, they eventually cease practicing the Catholic faith, thinking they missed the boat and it's not docking again in their lifetime.

Raymond hangs on to his Catholic identity by his fingernails. "I'm a Catholic. I don't want to be anything else," he explains. "I like what the church says, and I've always gone to Mass. But this is getting to be ridiculous." Raymond spent most of his life in active urban environments—Atlanta, New York, Chicago, San Francisco, or wherever his parents, and later his job, took him. But his last move dropped him in the middle of a diocese "an hour from nowhere," with relatively few options for church attendance. "I'm used to great music, great celebration, a real lively bunch of people," he laments. "I'm used to *hip* church. But now I've got screechy singers and a preacher who has nothing good to say, and I'm saddled with God's 'frozen' people where God's 'chosen' people used to be. I don't know how much longer I can take this. I'd be better off staying home. At least I wouldn't end up mad as all get-out every Sunday morning."

Raymond's in a tough situation. Are there jobs Catholics can't take, and places Catholics can't live, if they take their relationship to the church seriously? The truth is, according to the laws of the church, the laity has a *right* to good liturgy, and there shouldn't be dull, dead, or bad parishes. But church leaders are human, and not all pastors have the right stuff. And let's face it: not every Catholic wants what Raymond wants from the church. It could be that plenty of people who live "an hour from nowhere" are quite happy with the community that is challenging Raymond's commitment.

FINDING YOURSELF ON THE MAP

These stories from the lives of alienated Catholics are all true. And all of them are significant and worthy of concern on the part of the church. It is impossible to be comprehensive about the ways people may find themselves distanced from their Catholic identity, but hopefully this survey has given you some pegs on which to hang your own particular situation. A crisis of belief or theology; injustice; lack of hospitality; liturgies that seem boring and not connected to a direct experience of God or to the joys and problems people face in their lives; a sense of too much structure, of meaning derived from rote repetition, of a church more concerned with its leaders than with the bulk of its people; priests and other ministers who don't seem to have the time for people who come to them or who don't exercise enough patience or sensitivity; lack of information or bad information; life changes—these reasons and others cause people to feel that the church has little to say to them, cares more about itself than them, and not only does not lead them to God but gets in the way of a relationship with God.

Many alienated Catholics feel a sharp sense of pain over the conflict between the church they love and ways they may have been treated or ignored by church members or representatives. Those who feel a deep connection to the Mass or value being part of an ancient tradition find nonetheless that they cannot tolerate other aspects of their church experience and are wounded by the choice to separate from it. Their loss is our loss, the *church's* loss, and theirs is an injury that demands a healing solution and at least the opportunity for reconciliation.

Until very recently, lots of sincere and well-intentioned Catholics have questioned their church membership without recourse to satisfying answers and have simply moved on, unnoticed and without much effort on the part of the official church to find out why. But other Catholics, clergy and laypeople alike, *have* noticed, *have* listened, and feel an obligation and desire to offer support, encouragement, and any assistance that might be sought to those who have been marginalized by their experience of church in any way. If the church has failed you, if *we* have failed you, we are truly sorry and ask your forgiveness. And if at all possible, we'd like to offer some thoughts about what can be done to build a bridge across the separation or what *should* have been done the first time around in your life with the church.

THREE

What Good Is the Church?

Some folks, both within and outside of organized religion, wonder what the heck you need a church for anyway. If the point of religion is to foster a relationship with God, this mammoth amount of institution, structure, dogma, and ritual can seem excessive, maybe even in the way of its own intended goal. The enterprise of church, any church, hangs on the precarious, limited, faulty efforts of human beings, prone to sin and error like ourselves. Why should we follow them or listen to any authority beyond the dictates of our own conscience? History has proved that the lumbering institution of religion in general, and Catholicism in particular, has gotten it wrong many times throughout the centuries. We don't have to go farther than the Crusades, the inquisitions, or the still cloudy initial response of the church during the Second World War to see that following the lead of church officials could be disastrous or deadly in certain circumstances. Tragically, the clergy scandals of recent times and the enabling role played by the bishops reveal only too sharply that just because the church makes a decision doesn't mean the decision is beyond reproach.

In light of this reality, a person might well consider following another religious path—say, a less centrally governed form of Christianity, like a congregational assembly, which has more freedom to adapt to local circumstances. One might also choose to fashion a personalized spiritual journey as he or she goes along. As even churchgoing folk will often admit, a walk in the woods can be as inspiring and "spiritual" an experience as sitting in church for an hour. So why not abandon church in favor of the Sierra Club? Others might prefer to stay at home and read their Bibles privately or follow their own more meaningful prayer practices: yoga, meditation, a feminist-modified ritual, a male drum-banging group, charismatic prayer circles, or any of the many more practices people can use.

Any of these spiritual routes can add a great deal of life-giving energy to those who choose them, and none of them are objectively harmful. Of course, people often find that "escaping" the Catholic Church doesn't guarantee a solution to the problems of religion altogether. As sociologist Father Andrew Greeley has observed, what many Protestants discovered as a result of the Reformation is that it does no good to leave the church. Most of the conflicts identified in the first two chapters of this book would get nods of recognition from Christians of every denomination and persuasion!

But does leaving the confines of organized religion or at least Christianity lead to perfect serenity in spiritual practice? A woman in San Francisco who is a ranking leader in a New Age religious movement admitted privately to a Christian friend that "all of the pettiness, the power-mongering, the jostling for position and back-stabbing you'd expect in traditional religious hierarchies exist here too. You'd think at least we pagans would be free of it!" The problem, it would appear, is not religion per se, but human nature itself.

So maybe the back-to-nature approach to spirituality is the only free route, steering clear of groups and clubs and membership entirely. Well, even there we won't be totally safe from codes and regulations (don't forget to pack out your trash), debates about personal practice (vegetarian, vegan, or "vile meat eater"?), and the occasional clash of interests (canned music in the campground, those partying till dawn, and inconsiderate hikers shatter the ideal pretty readily).

The truth is, if we're going to live in a world with other people in it (so far there are few alternatives to this) and pursue a path of goodness, growth, and wholeness or "holiness" while we're here (elements of the spiritual journey), it might be helpful, even wise, to find a way to do that together. That's basically what church is all about.

FACING THE FOUR QUESTIONS

Before we take on the meaning of church, however, it would be good to have the "God talk." A conversation about *God* and *religion* can be a slippery business because what one person means by those words may be different from what the next person understands them to mean. For example, some people automatically think of miracles when they hear the phrase "acts of God." Other people, just as quickly, start listing natural disasters!

To create a framework for meaningful conversation on these issues, a whole profession is hard at work in every generation in order to make the "God talk" easier. These are the theologians of every religious tradition. They can be really intimidating to read directly because scholars are used to talking to each other, and they often use German or Latin even when they're writing in English! (And if it's all Greek to you, we should mention that they also use a lot of Greek and Hebrew, the original languages of the Bible.) But you don't have to read the big names in theology, folks like Sts. Augustine and Thomas Aquinas or recent lights like Karl Rahner and Monika Hellwig, to make use of what theologians are saying about God. You can "do theology" yourself, right in the privacy of your own home. In fact, you already do, even if you're not aware of it.

Every human soul wrestles sooner or later with four big questions:

Who is God?

Who am I?

What is the goal of life?

How should I live to achieve that goal?

As soon as we engage those questions, we are plunged into the heart of the enterprise of theology.

Who Is Your God?

Even if we don't believe in the existence of a deity, we still have a God (or god, or multiple gods) that governs the motivation of *our* existence. Even if the word *God* never crosses our lips, we have a central person or thing or objective we serve with all of our best intentions.

So how do we go about unraveling our personal theology? For a Christian the first of the four big questions (Who is God?) might be answered simply: God is the almighty Creator of the Judeo-Christian tradition, the God of the Bible, the Father of Jesus and the Lord of my life. Other faith traditions or spiritual paths would answer according to their teachings: God is the God of the covenant with Abraham, Isaac, Jacob, and their descendents. God is Allah. God is Being. God is wisdom or enlightenment. God is Goddess. God is bliss, or nothingness, or everything.

For people who are not consciously pursuing a religious quest, the question still must be answered. Some of the answers, whether or not they are ever intentionally expressed, are evident in where our passion lies: God is my immediate family, which must be sustained and protected no matter what the cost. God is security, personal freedom, happiness, my job. God is the pursuit of wealth, fame, self-actualization, or power. God may be romantic love or sex. God may take the form of an addiction, like alcohol or narcotics or gambling or food. God may also be "the cause," which could be human rights, serving the poor, fighting the war, or fighting against war.

To figure out which God you serve, all you have to do is examine your life. Who or what demands your allegiance before all else? Where does the bulk of your passion and energy go? What would be the last thing you would be willing to sacrifice, or for what would you be willing to die? How do you use most of your time? What are your most unshakable values and your deepest longings?

Sometimes our answers to these questions may surprise us. Maybe we thought our God is the one we talk about in church, but the truth may be that our own comfort or ambition is the real God we are committed to serving. As Jesus once phrased it, "No one can serve two masters" (Mt 6:24 NRSV). We may give lip service to God in heaven, but much of the time we are humbled to realize that we are more dedicated to serving ourselves here on earth.

Are You Who You Think You Are?

The second question we are all asking, whether we are conscious of it or not, concerns our identity: who am I? Most of us accept that young people are going to be about the business of "finding themselves," but we may like to think that the search for identity is all wrapped up by age twenty-one. Some of us go so far as to admit that a second-tier "identity check" is occasionally necessary in midlife: hence the midlife crisis. It is probably more accurate to think of identity as a fluid process, always being tinkered with on one level or another throughout life. Each role we take on, every move we make, each new event that engulfs us, and every decision we consider brings us to a crossroads where we redefine who we are and what we're really about.

So many elements form and re-form who we are! Our education—whether academic, professional, or the ongoing lessons of life—obviously shapes how we understand ourselves and the world we live in. If we fall in love or experience loneliness or choose a lone road deliberately, each of these factors affects how we know ourselves. If we marry, have children, divorce, remain single, or come to terms with a gay identity, any of these relationship-orienting positions has great consequences for our self-acceptance and sense of purpose. If we live in our hometown forever, move across the country or into another culture entirely, or reach across racial or religious or class lines, we may find our understanding of who we are radically altered by these choices. What we do professionally or what we do with our time if we are not in the workforce is of great importance to how we view ourselves. Acquiring or losing financial security, status, or power, and other shifts in our place within society dramatically influence our self-perception. Changes in our health or ability and the death of those we love or depend on can lead to overnight reevaluations of who we are and what our life is about.

The matter of identity is crucial to us. Being male or female; black or white or Asian or Hispanic; native-born or newcomer; rich or poor; Jewish or Muslim or Christian; old or young; intellectually gifted or challenged; gay or straight; blind or sighted; famous or obscure—all of these elements are pertinent to how we go about living our lives. But identity becomes a *religious* question, a *theological* question, when we recognize that all of the useful energy of our lives goes into the service of who or what our God is.

Because of this, when we answer the first of the four big questions, in a way we have already answered the rest.

In other words, who *I* am and understand myself to be is largely determined by who I think *God* is. For example, if God in my estimation is the great judge of the universe, who ultimately deems me worthy or unworthy (and will snatch me up to heaven or cart me off to hell based on certain principles well outlined in the Ten Commandments or elsewhere), then my basic self-understanding is that I am "judged." My whole life, whether I like it or not, will be shaped according to this central governing principle. God is the judge, and I am either saved or damned by how I live up to the precepts of this immutable and unavoidable presence awaiting me at the end of time. If this God is *my* God, then whatever else I may be is evaluated through that fundamental lens. If God is the judge, then the way I see myself in my personal relationships (in my marriage, divorce, or homosexuality), in all of my failings or virtues (good provider for my family, alcoholic, churchgoer, absent parent), and at whatever stage in my life (young adult with career questions, or facing sudden illness, or very old) turns like a kaleidoscope on that primary axis.

There are innumerable answers to who God is and who we are in response. God may be wrathful, paternal, distant, or absent, to name a few. We may identify our own role as judgmental, childlike, abandoned, or indifferent as a result.

On the other hand—and thank God there is another hand, or many hands, to consider—if "God is love," as St. John says simply (1 Jn 4:8 NRSV), then who are we revealed to be by that answer? We are "beloved." We are the ones whom God loves, those created out of love and for the sake of love. Imagine how we live out of *that* identity, given every factor that otherwise shapes our self-understanding. Have we been inadequate parents? Did we steal or lie or cheat or harm others to get where we are? Are we basically good people with run-of-the-mill flaws: impatience, jealousy, greed, laziness? Are we sexually irresponsible? Have we failed to love God or others? If God is the God who loves us, then that love may yet be our salvation. As St. Paul said, love "bears all things, believes all things, hopes all things, endures all things. Love never fails" (1 Cor 13:7–8 NAB). Wouldn't it be wonderful to live out of the certainty that *all* of our human failures cannot put us beyond the love of God, which does not fail?

What Is the Goal of Life?

At this point, you can see how answering the first of the four big questions really has an impact on your response to all of them. Who God is and who we are determine what the point in living in this world really is, which brings us to the third question: what is the goal of life? If God is money, as it is for some folks, then we define ourselves in the acquisition of money. The goal of our lives becomes clear: to get more. This goal will likely crowd out some others, like our attention to a spouse or children, or personal development. It may even bring us to compromise certain moral principles that get in the way, like honesty or fairness. The God we serve, whether God above or a lesser deity below, requires our hearts.

Some people do live, consciously or unconsciously, in service to a lesser deity, which is a form of "idolatry," to use the Judeo-Christian term. But other forms of idolatry may not be materialistic. For some, God might be the attainment of wisdom or knowledge. These are good to pursue in themselves, but to make knowledge your God can be crippling and even arrogant. Not to take anything away from the virtue of science, but some aspects of reality remain veiled in infinite mystery not apprehensible by limited mortals, and to believe the universe can be controlled utterly

will prove disappointing. As the writer of Ecclesiastes said, a lifetime of learning for its own sake may lead one to conclude that it's
all "vanity and a chasing after wind" (Eccl 1:14 NRSV). That
doesn't prevent some rationally minded folks from putting all their
eggs in the knowledge basket. A junior professor once said to her
student with absolute seriousness, "If I don't get my doctorate, I
can't respect myself. I would never be happy. It's essential." Such
persons value the degrees and credentials and the climb up the
professional ladder as confirmations that they are gaining ground
in the acquisition of learning. Others may not want the degrees,
but they are still eager to "know." They read voraciously, or gain
control of the information in their work environment, or work their
way inside the loops and corridors of privileged information. They
have to feed their brains, to know what's going on, and their only
satisfaction is the sense of mastery that comes with knowing more
than most people about *something*.

Answering the goal question is critical because we naturally
orient ourselves in relationship to our goals. If our goal in this
world is to please, to be found worthy (of our parents, our spouse,
a mentor, or God), then life becomes a juggling act of keeping all
the worthiness factors in the air: obedience, meeting expectations,
producing success of one sort or another, or moral perfection. If we
do something we think will displease this God, we'll try to hide it
from our Father or Mother in heaven or on earth, and perhaps even
from ourselves. If we are "caught" in our sin, then we may feel the
abandonment or loss of security that children experience when
they fear they have lost the affection of the people they depend on
for their survival.

For those of us who have discovered God through the revelation of Jesus Christ, we may identify God as the compassionate
healer, the teacher of wisdom, the one willing to lay down his life

for his friends. We might then identify ourselves as the recipients of great love, who have been found worthy of healing, instruction, friendship, and great sacrifice. How would we define the goal of life under these circumstances? Perhaps the fundamental response could be summed up in the word *grateful*. We might be drawn to return friendship with friendship and to demonstrate loyalty and honesty in our relationship with God. If God is who Jesus says God is, then the goal of life is to celebrate the goodness that has been given to us and to share it with others.

How Should We Live?

At this point the "mathematics" of theology seems pretty clear. You plug in the first response to the equation, and the rest of the numbers add up naturally. Once we answer the first question (Who is God?) honestly, then personal identity, the goal of life, and what we should do to attain that goal are surprisingly clear.

So when we come to the final question (How should I live?), the answer is already implied in our first three responses. The person for whom "God and country" are more or less synonymous will be a staunch patriot. The goal for that person would be the welfare and defense of the homeland and its values before all else. That person may feel strongly about having the flag displayed in church, going to war as an acceptable form of global problem solving, investing in the economy, policymaking that holds "America first," taking the position "my country, right or wrong," and so on. A life of integrity would demand such consistency, if one's God is to be served.

If we follow the God described by the prophets of Scripture, then our response to "How should I live?" shifts a bit. In Scripture God is not identified with country but offers instead a regular and radical critique of it. This God did choose a particular nation,

Israel, as a personal possession—but many of us don't live in Israel today, nor are we Jewish. This same God also made it known that *all* nations would come to serve and honor the name of the Lord (Is 61:11), that all the earth belongs to God (Ps 24:1), that salvation is available to all regardless of nationality (Rom 3:21–24), and that the great desire of God's heart is to assume all things in Christ so that at the end of time God will be all in all (1 Cor 15:28). Clearly, the God of Scripture makes pure nationalism a difficult stance to defend. The God of peace and justice revealed by Isaiah is the champion of every nation and tongue.

God's universal concern becomes even more explicit in the revelation of the New Testament. Jesus came for the house of Israel, but he also healed outsiders when his mercy was called upon, including the enemies of his nation (Mt 8:5–13, 15:22–28). Jesus taught that God's justice was wielded first and foremost for the disadvantaged—who were often sinners (prostitutes, the sick, and the mentally ill, as they were defined then), traitors (tax collectors), foreigners (Samaritans and Romans), and other undesirables—not for the properly defined "good guys." Everyone expected that Jesus came to bring peace to his occupied nation and would run the Romans out of town, but Jesus promised to bring the sword to every household, causing anguish within families (Lk 12:51–53).

If our God is the biblical God of justice and peace, then who are we, what's the goal, and how should we live? We are advocates for justice, voices raised on behalf of the poor, willing to share our resources and cast our votes for "the least of these . . ." (Mt 25:40 NRSV). We will have to consider any act of aggression or declaration of war as indefensible in all but a handful of circumstances. Sometimes this may put us at odds with the goals of our own family, community, or country because we are citizens of a higher kingdom, not of this world (Jn 18:36). How we will live to attain the goals of justice and peace may be surprising, sometimes personally costly, often requiring courage and maybe even heroism. We may have to make personal sacrifices, we may march or go to jail, we may not rise to the top of our professions or gain the seats of power, and we will probably never be rich. Celebrity will probably elude us—though we have a good shot at notoriety.

From here you can do your own theology to see where your answers are taking you. If you choose to follow the God revealed in Jesus—the compassionate healer, teacher, and friend we spoke of earlier—your life journey will be enfolded in God's kindness and beneficence. You can approach God in times of injury, trusting in God's power and desire to heal you. You may become a student of wisdom, reading the Bible and absorbing truthful teaching wherever you hear it, testing it against the truth of Jesus. You will naturally be a friend to others, especially the poor, and perhaps find yourself laying down your life by degrees out of a love that is overwhelming.

We can only give what we have. We can only be what our God is. We become what we serve. This is why religious questions, properly understood, are fundamentally life questions, and we answer them with all that we are and will be.

SO WHAT'S THEOLOGY GOT TO DO WITH CHURCH?

Life questions tend to start out personal: who is my God, and who am I in light of that? But they quickly become interpersonal: what's the goal of my life, and how do I live that out in the world around me? Try as we might to be one, no one is an island; no one is even a *peninsula*. Most of us are pretty landlocked in our relationships, in a sort of perpetual heartland of commitments and obligations. If the Bible is to be trusted, then that's as it should be. God did not think it was good for us to be alone (Gn 2:18). We were designed with relationship in mind, it seems. And if God is love and we are made in the likeness of God (Gn 1:27), then we are essentially love too. *Love* is a verb. It exists in its expression and not in theory. If we are made for love, and if we're going to express it, we need one another.

So community is not just an ideal; it's a necessity. That becomes clear with a quick glance at the Bible. The story of Scripture is as much about the community of the faithful as it is about God. We might say the two main characters in the Bible are God and us. The Bible can be seen as an ongoing study in weaving theology: who is God, and who are we in light of that understanding? God's identity is explored in several significant stages of humanity's awareness of the divine: as creator of the universe, as the one who promises us a home and a place to belong, as the savior who delivers us from slavery to freedom and gives us a law to bind us closer to the divine will, and as the word spoken through the prophets to guide and challenge us. In the Christian story God takes one more entirely unprecedented step in revealing divinity to humanity: God takes on flesh and accepts our fate in being tempted by sin, vulnerable to suffering, and limited by death. And in accepting the terms of our humanity, God expands them, breaking through the bonds of sin, death, and despair, and opening for us the possibility of eternal life and joy.

In a nutshell, that's the Bible. But what we do with that story is how we become "biblical people" ourselves. The drama isn't over. It didn't end at the cross, or with the resurrection or ascension of Jesus. In a certain sense, the drama *begins* there for us because the Bible launches right into the story of the church, which is the story we are invited to share.

Where does the church come from? It emerges from that continuing stream of biblical narration about God and the people of

God. First, God created the world and entered into relationship with it, specifically with humanity as a unique image of divinity capable of friendship with God. Later God forged a commitment (called the covenant) with Abraham and Sarah and their descendants. And later, through the law of Moses and the kingship of David, God continued to invite the nation closer and closer to the heart of divine love. But as we know from the story, not to mention the world around us, most people didn't accept the invitation. So God sent prophets, early and often, to caution and cajole the people to turn from the direction in which they were moving. Few heeded God's messengers, and the relationship was strained to the point of alienation and exile from the land God had promised his people. But throughout history the story of God and humanity remains an unbroken narrative, and when Jesus arrives on the scene, the story just gets broader and more universal. This is where the church comes in.

The first "church," we might say, is the band of twelve followers that Jesus gathers around him. Twelve is a symbolic number, important because it represents the twelve original tribes of Israel or "all the people," as the storytellers intended. But the group also contained others, including the women who followed Jesus from Galilee throughout his ministry (Lk 23:49), people like Susanna and Joanna, who used their own resources to support the work Jesus was doing (Lk 8:1–3). From what we know of this first church, it was hardly an ideal community. Andrew, one of the Twelve, was a "career" disciple; he had followed John the Baptist before Jesus. Professional groupies like this are not always terribly dependable, one eye always cocked for the next big movement to come along. Peter, Andrew's brother, was a natural leader, but he had some serious weaknesses: impetuousness, sometimes speaking or acting before his brain was engaged (Mt 16:22–23). And he had a distinct lack of nerve in the matter of follow-through. He accepted

Jesus' invitation to walk on water and then chickened out (Mt 14:28–31). He swore he'd follow Jesus to the death but then denied Jesus vigorously when his life was on the line (Mt 26:33–35, 69–75). Thomas, we know, wanted proof positive before he committed to his faith (Jn 20:25). Mrs. Zebedee, the mother of James and John, followed Jesus around in part to be sure that her sons got top billing in the kingdom to come (Mt 20:21). And Judas, as it turns out, was the most dangerous element of the inner circle. This was the first church, and it was a bit of a disaster all around.

THE CHURCH GETS SPIRIT

If Jesus in the flesh didn't establish a perfect community on earth, it should not come as a shock that the present church is not exactly a model community. Sometimes Christians point to the "ideal" early church with a sigh, wishing to return to the good old days, when the apostles spoke the gospel courageously and everyone surrendered their goods to the common purpose. If we read the Acts of the Apostles and then St. Paul's letters more closely, we see that the "ideal" early church wasn't ideal. Peter and Paul argued about policy regarding the inclusion of gentile outsiders in the church. Paul goes so far as to call Peter ("Kephas" in the text) a hypocrite (Gal 2:11–14). There were snubs between Jewish Christians divided by language: Greek-speaking Jews didn't get as much as Hebrew-speaking Jews in the daily distribution (Acts 6:1). The cultural context of the times interfered with the church's higher order of business: Could women be incorporated into the community equally, when they were not equals in society? What should be done about slaves who were baptized? Were Jewish and non-Jewish Christians to be treated the same, and how could they eat at the same table, which was forbidden by Jewish law? The early church, by its own account, had wrinkles in its fabric, and in the writings of the New Testament it becomes clear that not all the wrinkles were successfully ironed out in the first generations.

Still, this same church was the recipient of the Holy Spirit at Pentecost. Pentecost made heroes out of cowards and eloquent preachers out of poor fishermen. Suddenly the gifts of preaching, teaching, healing, and exorcism were alive in a community that had run away when Jesus was arrested. The apostles now spoke boldly in the streets, able to face the religious leaders, and even kings and Roman rulers, with great authority. It was a startling transformation and one that could only come about through divine intervention, by which we mean not divine manipulation but divine inspiration. The spirit of God, which Jesus had promised to bestow on his church, now dwelled in the assembly of believers. The Spirit's gifts of wisdom, understanding, knowledge, counsel, courage, reverence, and wonder in God's presence were active in their midst (1 Cor 12:4–11; see also Is 11:2–3). The fruits of that same Spirit— love, joy, peace, patience, kindness, generosity, faithfulness, gentleness, and self-control—were the product of lives given over to the Spirit's authority (Gal 5:22–23). It was an exciting time to be a disciple!

The other really exciting time to be a disciple is right now. In fact, *now* is the only time when discipleship has any real hope of engaging the Holy Spirit and unleashing God's power and grace into our world again. As St. Paul said, "See, now is the acceptable time; see, now is the day of salvation!" (2 Cor 6:2 NRSV). This is the hour that is given to us, and if we are at all serious about following Jesus, this is the time to do it.

The Holy Spirit isn't a relic of the church's past, some curiosity to view in a museum of religious artifacts. The power of the Holy Spirit was promised to the church by no less a person than Jesus, who pledged that this authority would remain with his church (Jn 14:16), just as he would till the end of time (Mt 28:20). Jesus knew human nature literally from the inside out. He knew our flaws and the relentless tug of evil on our hearts. He knew that sin would be the death of us if not for the forgiveness of God. Jesus did not expect that his followers would ever get their acts together on their initiative alone. We do this only through God's goodness and the free gift of grace. The Spirit is our guide on the road out—literally the "exodus"—from sin's crushing impact on our lives and relationships.

The church remains the community with whom we take that exodus journey out of human darkness. The church is where we celebrate God's presence in "word" and "sacrament"—that is, in the story of God's people we listen to in Scripture and the meal we share that binds our lives to God and each other on this journey. It is here that we learn how to love and practice the art of forgiveness when we fall short of love's ideal. This is our call, our invitation.

CATHOLICISM'S UNIQUE TREASURE

Jews and Christians alike share the story of God's people in the Old Testament. Christians of every denomination likewise hold the Gospels and the New Testament in common, as well as centuries of history and testimony to the faith of the apostles. But Catholicism adheres to the idea that human beings benefit not only from "story" but also from "signs" that can be seen and touched. That's why we celebrate seven sacraments that open windows onto the world of grace we can hold in our hands. Sacraments are not rituals that God needs to bring grace to us but signs that *we* need to see what we are saying about God's grace. Our identity as the free people of God (baptism); the confirmation of the Spirit at work in us (confirmation); our unity in the body of Christ (Eucharist); God's compassion (penance or reconciliation); God's healing (anointing of the sick); and the blessing of our love (matrimony) and our service (holy orders) are seven moments lifted out of all of life to celebrate the mystery of God's love for us in *every* hour and circumstance.

This sense of the sacred made available in humble signs is present in our prayer and ritual practices, like the rosary, stations of the cross, meditation before the crucifix or the tabernacle, lighting vigil candles, wearing ashes, and getting our throats blessed. We also honor holiness as it was demonstrated in the lives of committed disciples of Jesus known as the saints. Since it was not beneath God's dignity to assume our humanity but was in fact part of the divine plan for God to be known to us in this way, we make use of tangible and earthly things to come to God with confidence.

In this chapter we have offered a lightning-quick survey of why participating in a church is useful, even imperative, in the life of faith. We have considered how the quest of religion puts us in touch with our identity, purpose, and the meaning of our lives, and gives us direction in how to live. We have looked at how the biblical story of God's people is part of the continuing narrative of the present community of the church. And we have offered a few thoughts on how Catholicism uniquely expresses the gift of grace that Jesus revealed to his disciples in sending the Holy Spirit. We hope that these ideas will help to highlight why being a member of the community of faith is or would be meaningful to you. Though we often and understandably get bogged down in the church institution of our particular generation, the gift of *being* church is something that is meant to awaken faith and sustain it. If you think this common journey is still of value to you in some way, the next chapter will assist in sorting out some options for continuing the conversation.

FOUR

What Do You Want from the Church?

Having had the conversation about alienation with family members and friends ourselves, it is no surprise to us that some people will read the title of this chapter and reply immediately and emphatically, "Nothing!" It is instinctive to want to put distance between ourselves and the source of pain or conflict. But it is also just as basic for human beings to want to resolve matters that continue to cause heartache and aggravation. If there is a way through this difficult terrain, many would be grateful to find it.

Other factors may lead us to look for solutions to the problem of church estrangement. It's not just that hurt and anger and unaddressed spiritual hunger are uncomfortable feelings to harbor and we'd prefer not to feel this way. We may also still want something from the church, despite all the water that's gone under the bridge; and until things are straightened out, we're separated from the good things about our church as a result of what went bad.

In an even more fundamental sense, being at odds with the church may also make some of us feel a sense of distance in our relationship with God. If the church was the original avenue of our communication with God in prayer, sacrament, worship, and practice, finding that avenue blocked can put us at a disadvantage in this essential relationship. As St. Augustine once said, "Our hearts were made for You, O Lord, and they are restless, until they rest in You." We cannot afford to allow anything to jeopardize our primary experience of resting in God's care and compassion.

Thomas Merton, the celebrated writer-monk and adult convert to Catholicism who inspired a generation of young folks to reconsider the church, wrote stirringly about our common spiritual hunger in *New Seeds of Contemplation* (New York: New Directions, 1961, 183): "To desire God is the most fundamental of all human desires. It is the very root of all our quest for happiness." If your spiritual quest for happiness has been complicated by conflict in your relationship with the church, it may become imperative, for your peace of mind and wholeness, to assess and repair the damage. If reconciliation with the Catholic community is also desirable, it's never too late to move in that direction and begin the process of "coming home."

But before we can talk about what we want from the church, we have to step back a minute and consider what we mean by the word *church*. This may seem like an unnecessary side trip to make, at first. But as many of us have learned by revisiting this word, how we use it can make all the difference in the world.

ONE CHURCH, FIVE MEANINGS

What *is* church? Read the following statements thoughtfully and try to prioritize them from most central to least central according to what church means to you:

Church is where God always seems very real and close. The smell of incense, the sight of flickering candles, and the silence put me in touch with the sacred.

Being part of the church is important because the church is the keeper of Scripture, the sacraments, morality, and the faith.

We are the church, all of us together, and we come to know who Christ is in our celebration as a loving, faith-filled community.

Belonging to the church means accepting the commission to bring the gospel to all the world, not just keeping it to ourselves.

Being part of the church means embracing our true vocation, which is to teach, heal, serve, and forgive as Jesus did.

Remember, this is not a true-false quiz: all of the above reactions to the idea of church are valid. But many of us are naturally drawn to one or two of these facets of church more than the others. Hold this simple exercise in mind as you read through the chapter, and the next time you have a conversation with someone about the "church" listen to what is implied in each use of the word. When we discuss our relationship to the "church," we need to be aware that not everyone in the conversation means precisely the same thing by the use of that word.

Few folks would deny that at least one goal of religion is to help us get in touch with God and with what is holy by assisting us in seeing what is unseen. In this sense, we can think of the church as a *lens* that seeks to reveal the sacred in our midst. By the use of Scripture and sacrament, through the twin powers of story and symbol, the church essentially reveals Jesus Christ, who in turn shows God to us (see Jn 14:9). The church, then, is not ultimately about itself. When the church uses its unique gifts to make Jesus Christ real and present in the world, it achieves its purpose.

A lens, of course, can only focus on what you point it at. Many of the problems people have with the Catholic Church grow out of the ways in which the church becomes a distraction, obscuring or deviating from the gospel—the message it is supposed to deliver. At worst, the organizational aspects of the church can become *identified* with God instead of *illuminating* God for us. In this regard, the church gets in the way of those who are trying to see God and live as God intended us to live. The church becomes the picture, not the lens.

So it becomes obvious that our understanding of "church" will affect whether or not it is helpful or potentially harmful to us. Theologians have learned that even to have a conversation about the church, we must first all agree on its meaning; that is, which lens we are using and where we are aiming it. The issue is as old as the church itself, of course. In the New Testament we see Jesus naming Peter the rock upon which the church will stand (Mt 16:18). But later St. Paul identifies the church as the mystical body of believers with only one head, Christ himself (Col 1:18). These two statements are not intended to be in disagreement; but they use the term *church* in different ways. This is not surprising because the church is at once a human institution involving the likes of us as well as the "communion of saints," with membership stretching from here to the hereafter. We are at the same time saints *and* sinners, saved *and* in need of saving grace in every moment of the day. The church is human and divine, with its feet planted firmly on earth and its hands lifted to the heavens.

At the time of Vatican II in the 1960s, it was clear that the church as Catholics knew it was in the throes of a great hour of renewal. At the summons of Pope John XXIII, theologians and church leaders came from all over the world to discuss what kinds of changes the church was facing and how they should be implemented to best serve the church's mission in the world. One theologian at the council, a Jesuit named Avery Dulles, started recording instances of the use of the word *church* and what the speaker intended by it. He observed that some of the tension and conflict among various positions stemmed from the fact that people meant different things when using that simple but multifaceted term.

This led Father Dulles to write an influential book in 1974 titled *Models of the Church*. In it he looked at the Catholic Church from five different angles reflecting the meanings he had been hearing from church leaders. First, he explored the church as an *institution*, or organizational structure carrying church wisdom and practice forward in every generation. Next he considered the church as a *mystery* uniting us more profoundly with the heart of the great mystery, which is God. He looked at the church's mission to be a *herald*, the bearer of the good news of Jesus. He examined the church's call to be a *community*, a "sacrament" in action and an assembly of celebration. Finally, Dulles viewed the church as a *servant* that embraces the challenge of discipleship and does what Jesus did. None of these models by itself describes the whole church, of course, but each describes a facet of it; each is a way of looking at what the church is and does. When these different dimensions of the church work together in balance and harmony, the church functions pretty well. But when one of the elements is overemphasized to the detriment of others, it can throw the focus of the lens seriously out of whack.

A closer examination of these five models can help us to locate ourselves within the spectrum of church and perhaps to articulate more accurately what we might still value in our relationship with the community of faith.

THE CHURCH AS INSTITUTION: THE GATEKEEPER

Greg became a Catholic at the time of his marriage ten years ago. He was already a Christian, so expressing his faith in a new way wasn't much of a problem for him. He discovered that he liked the celebration of the Mass and found the people he met in the parish to be sincere, dedicated, and enlivened by their beliefs. But still, a decade later, he's not so sure he'd stay Catholic five more minutes if it weren't for his wife. "The church makes me nuts," he admits. "All these rules and traditions, and the top-heavy Vatican structure, and the decisions made centuries ago that won't go away."

When Greg *goes* to church, there's no problem, but when he talks about the church, he has a litany of complaints. Clearly, he means more than one thing by "church," and it's the second meaning that causes him distress. Greg's problem isn't the Sunday morning encounter but the government, or institution, of the church.

The *institutional* dimension of the church refers to the organization that keeps Catholicism as we know it afloat. Like any other vast structure, the church is governed by both people and rules. The people are known as the hierarchy, including the pope, cardinals, and bishops. On the local parish level, we also have priests, deacons, and sometimes very aggressive parish secretaries. (Just kidding about the secretaries.) The rules come in various kinds, ranging from canon law, which is the law of the church, to the *Catechism of the Catholic Church,* which contains a comprehensive statement of church teaching. Above all, Catholicism seeks to govern itself according to the teachings and authority of Christ. The church derives its leadership authority from the apostles through the laying on of hands, practiced in the sacrament of holy orders. Its teaching tradition likewise comes from this apostolic source, which is added to in every generation.

The institutional features of the church can be described by factors common to most organizations: administration, governance, and order. Objectively speaking, these are benign elements; employed with wisdom, they hold a positive value. For any worthwhile thing to be shared between two people, much less between generations, it has to undergo a certain amount of standardization and agreement. How else do we make commitments, coexist in neighborhoods, keep families together, or even play a game of stickball? For the gospel to make it from the first generation to the next, some version of the story needed to be agreed upon and set down in writing. As the community grew and spread, more decisions needed to be made and judgments on conflicts determined, and they too were written down. There is always a dance in history between the need to stabilize an institution so that it can remain the treasury of good and the equally pressing need to move the institution forward so that it can remain nimble. The longer an institution exists, the larger and more elaborate its structure tends to become. The dance becomes richer but also more complex and liable to misstep.

It is fair to say that the gospel would not have made it through twenty centuries without the church. That is why the institutional church is almost synonymous with the very idea of "church." When people use the term *church* casually, the institutional church is generally the meaning they intend. When people talk about *leaving* the church, it's almost always the institutional church to which they are referring. Since administering law and hierarchy, ritual and morality, is what the institution does, this gatekeeper aspect of church is the one that most seems to push, offend, or put folks beyond its membership according to its own principles. Certainly, it is part of the purpose of an institution to define its membership. If you want to know if you're in or you're out, the principles of the organization offer clear demarcations of its boundaries and of what is "beyond the pale."

Some Catholics will automatically think of the precepts or commandments of the church here. These precepts convey the basic rules Catholics are to follow as members of the church. It is interesting to note that historically the precepts are derived from four principles put forth by the first church council in Jerusalem (see Acts 15). The present form of the precepts has been around since the Middle Ages and has varied between five and six in number, depending on whose listing you followed. Most of us learned that we had these six obligations as Catholics: (1) to keep holy Sunday and holy days of obligation by attending Mass and refraining from work; (2) to keep the days of fast and abstinence appointed by the church; (3) to go to confession at least once a year; (4) to receive communion at least once a year at Easter time; (5) to contribute to the support of one's pastor; and (6) to observe the laws of the church regarding marriage. In the present *Catechism of the Catholic Church,* the sixth precept is dropped entirely, and the first precept is separated into one rule regarding Sundays and another rule involving holy days. The fifth precept, about supporting your pastor, is now included as an additional "duty" but downgraded from an outright commandment. (See nos. 2041–2043 in the *Catechism* for the new wording.) The precepts, however they are worded, call on Catholics to participate in the celebrations of the sacraments with great thoughtfulness and commitment. None of them, when you think about it, is an unusual request for those who claim membership in the church.

The catechism calls these precepts "obligatory" and "positive" (no. 2041); that is, they tell us what to do in order to claim our Catholic identity rather than what not to do to keep from losing it. Keeping these precepts, the catechism explains, is meant to "guarantee to the faithful the indispensable minimum in the spirit of prayer and moral effort, in the growth in love of God and neighbor" (no. 2041). In other words, the precepts ask for a certain minimum of participation in the life of the church, setting the barest of requirements for membership in the church and, hopefully, laying the foundation for greater participation.

Let's look at one more statement from the institutional side of the church that offers a definition of what it means to be Catholic. Out of Vatican II came a series of documents that expressed the teaching of the church; among them was *Lumen Gentium* (*Light of Nations,* 1964), which explained the meaning of the church itself. One section of the document deals with the "Catholic faithful." It says that, through faith and baptism, people enter the church and accept what it stands for and what holds it together: the profession of the creed, the sacraments, communion, and the hierarchy—pope and bishops—through whom Christ guides the church. Like the precepts, this listing of essential elements of a Catholic identity is intended as "helps" for those of us who wonder whether we're in or we're out. If you read the Nicene Creed and find yourself in agreement with it, if the sacraments are meaningful and valuable to you, and if you accept the authority of the church (at least per se— and we aren't talking about accepting every word that comes from the mouth of Father Sid in particular), then you are already more Catholic than you may have thought.

Certainly, the Catholic Church—like any religious body or secular organization—defines what it expects from its members. It has a right to do so, and it needs to do so for the sake of integrity.

But the problem with having "membership rules" becomes obvious at once: some people may settle for the least common denominator of membership, following the rules and no more. The precepts and Vatican II guidelines are meant to be the groundwork for greater involvement in the church. This invitation to participate may also exclude people who, despite a greater and more soulful commitment to the spirit of the church, find themselves on the outskirts of the community as a result of a conflict with or omission of some of these rules.

THE CHURCH AS MYSTERY: OUR UNION WITH GOD

What Erin wants from the church more than anything is to foster a genuine relationship with God. She doesn't come to church for the social life, and she's frankly uninterested in the political and sometimes fractious aspects of community. For her, faith is a quest to seek and find God, and religion is her vehicle for getting there. "Prayer, sitting before the tabernacle, and staying close to the sacraments helps me find my way," she says. "Life just gets so frantic out there, and when I feel anxious or confused or just exhausted, here is my peace, here is my center!"

Erin knows what the rest of us often forget: there's more to the business of church than meets the eye. The institutional aspect of church is so large, visible, and compelling that we are often tempted to stop there and say it *is* the church, period. But the institution is the earthly and tangible expression of the church's authority. On the celestial and more profound side of Christian belief is the recognition that the church is commissioned to be the Body of Christ and sharers in his life, in this world and the next. Significantly fewer Catholics who leave the church intend to leave *this* identity behind them. The mystery of our union with God in the life of Christ is the most precious gift of faith and the one that gives the institutional church its meaning and its mission. It should also be said that the mystical body of the church includes all Christians in its embrace, not just Catholics.

Body of Christ is a term layered with meanings. It describes the ways Jesus remains present to us in his resurrection, in the Eucharist, and in the church throughout the ages. The Gospel stories of the resurrected Jesus (Lk 24 and Jn 20–21 in particular) reveal him interacting with his disciples beyond Easter Sunday and not as a ghost. Jesus appears not with the form of a resuscitated dead body but with a new, everlasting, glorified body. *Body of Christ* also refers to the real presence of Jesus in the Eucharist as Catholics understand it. In the celebration of the Mass, bread and wine become the real body and blood of Christ, now available to us as nourishing food and a source of our life in Christ. We also speak of the Body of Christ as the way in which Christ is present in his church and the way the members of the church relate to one another and to God. St. Paul writes, "For as in one body we have many members, . . . so we, who are many, are one body in Christ" (Rom 12:4–5 NRSV). Christ "is the head of the body, the church" (Col 1:18 NRSV). Together Christ and his members are truly one body, one spirit, one church.

Perhaps we focus on the institutional model of church so much because the mystical meaning of church can be so challenging to grasp. In fact, we *can't* grasp it because it is mystery: it deals with the unknowable and infinite nature of God. As Christians, we speak of our communion with God in the paschal mystery, by which we mean that we know God dwells in us because Jesus shared our suffering and death and invites us to share in his resurrected life. Jesus took on our humanity, and we become heirs of the eternal life of his divinity. The paschal mystery is the mystery of

how humanity and divinity meet and are held together in the person of Jesus Christ.

In every Eucharist, we celebrate with gratitude and joy that
Christ is eternally present in the church and in our world. This is
the transcendent moment of the mystical aspect of church. But the
mystery dimension of church also includes the larger quest for
holiness and union with God that inspires us. It involves the entire
Catholic heritage of prayer—spoken, silent, or sung; fixed or spontaneous; meditation and contemplation; our saying of the rosary
and walking the stations of the cross; our intercession for the dead
and blessing of the living. In other words, it involves our commitment to consecrating our world and our loved ones to God and our
journey of spiritual growth and the purification of our hearts to better know, love, and serve the God we seek.

Many Catholics who become disillusioned with the institutional church remain dedicated to the mystical communion of
Christ. In their prayer and perhaps their participation in another
form of Christian worship, they find union with God through
Christ a cherished and defining aspect of their life's purpose.

THE CHURCH AS HERALD: SPREADING THE WORD

Since joining the Wednesday night Bible study at her parish,
Deborah has been gripped by the immediacy and relevance of the
word of God. "It's like He's talking right to me, like the whole thing
has been written for my benefit," she says. Her attendance on
Sunday mornings has been spotty, and her prayers have been lukewarm most of her adult life. She has always felt the obligation to go
to church but never the kind of excitement she feels now on
Wednesday nights. "The Bible is so important!" she exclaims.

"And it's a gift from God's mouth to our ears. Why doesn't every Christian read their Bible every day?"

Deborah's got the fever, and Scripture has been known to have this effect on those who commit themselves to the message. The Bible contains the accumulated testimony of faith for Judeo-Christian believers, and there's nothing like a personal witness to touch our hearts and move us to examine our own lives. Bringing the gospel to all the world is what the church was founded for, and lighting hearts on fire is why the story was told and continues to be told.

So it should seem strange that the church as herald, or messenger of the Good News, is often thought of as a "Protestant" understanding of church. Catholics have often stereotyped themselves as the church of the sacraments and their Protestant sisters and brothers as the church of the Bible. There is some history behind this assumption, but it is also misleading. Although the Protestant Reformation of 1517 did ride on Martin Luther's words *sola scriptura* ("only Scripture") as its governing authority, many reformers, including John Calvin, recommended frequent reception of the Eucharist and did not question the belief that Holy Communion is the real presence of Christ. Many Protestant denominations continue to practice at least three sacraments: baptism, the Eucharist, and confirmation.

In the same way, although Catholicism adhered to the sacramental system and retained seven sacraments from the time of the Council of Trent (1545–1563), it never abandoned Scripture and remains committed to grounding all of its teachings in the word of God. But it is true to say that, after the time of the Reformation, Protestant thought was quite suspicious of images of God, Jesus, the Holy Spirit, and the saints, as well as any ritual that seemed to make the spiritual too concrete and manageable. Catholicism, for its part, swung far in the other direction, regarding the individual interpretation of Scripture to be subversive and corrosive to the unity of the church. So Catholics were often discouraged from reading the Bible for themselves, for fear they would misinterpret it and be led astray.

These days, however, many Protestants and Catholics have come closer to the center in their appreciation of sacrament and word. Both sign and story are seen as valuable witnesses to the presence of God at work in the world. So today we can speak of the herald model of church and mean the universal Christian commitment to spreading the good news of Christ. But let's not make the mistake of reducing the proclamation of the gospel to the usual stereotypes. The herald church isn't to be equated simply with Bible-thumping in the park, knocking on doors in the neighborhood, or the work of missionaries in far-off lands to bring Christianity where it isn't. Nor is it limited to quoting words from the Bible to those who (in our judgment) might need to hear them.

The real work of the herald is to testify to the truth of the gospel in word *and* action, in the way we live our lives and share our love. This naturally implies a life anchored in the Judeo-Christian story as it's told in the Bible. Scripture is powerful, as one New Testament writer emphasized: "The word of God is living and active, sharper than any two-edged sword" (Heb 4:12 NRSV). Immersing ourselves in this dynamic word in thoughtful study is the surest path to transformation of the heart and spirit. As St. John notes, the word of God became flesh in Jesus Christ (Jn 1:14). And once we incorporate that word, it becomes united with *our* flesh and *our* lives. As the ragged but true saying goes, you may be the only Bible someone else will ever read. What does the Scripture of your life reveal to others about what you believe and the God you serve?

Folks who become alienated from the church may do so because they've been "preached to death" by others—especially others who may not necessarily practice what they preach. This bludgeoning by word and hypocrisy in action are sincerely regrettable, as they fail to deliver the love of God to those who hunger and thirst for a living word to rouse their hearts. Far more people are attracted to the church because of the living word they encounter in people who have worked hard to become a mirror of God's good news in their words and in their love.

THE CHURCH AS COMMUNITY: GOD'S JOYFUL PEOPLE

The changes in the Mass after Vatican II were particularly hard on Cherie's grandmother. "Gram always liked to say her rosary during the Mass," Cherie says. "And suddenly there was all this hand-holding and greeting your neighbor going on every Sunday. She found it very distracting. Also, we got this new priest who wanted everybody to sign up for small faith-sharing groups. Gram didn't want any part of that! Her faith was a private business, between her and God and maybe the priest during confession. But she wasn't going to start 'forming community' with people she'd never sit down to dinner with otherwise."

By now the many layers of meaning involved when we speak of church should be coming into focus. What is the church? The institution that governs the faithful here on earth? The mystical Body of Christ through which we are united with God? The keeper and proclaimer of the gospel message? Yes, yes, and yes. But when we say "church," we also certainly refer to the community that is the repository of this faith. A few generations ago, some might have considered this meaning of *church* to be a "Protestant" use of the word. Protestants had community and fellowship; Catholics had the Mass, a solemn, formal celebration in Latin that discouraged interaction on a personal level. Since the time of the church renewal after Vatican II, more Catholic parishes have made an effort to defeat this stereotype and to encourage an atmosphere of genuine, interactive community. The decision to celebrate the Mass in the language of the people—making use of prayers, music, and cultural expressions appropriate to the local population—and the extended use of lay ministers in liturgy and parish roles created an environment more conducive to viewing the church as "a place for us" and not simply "God's house."

Vatican II affirmed the idea that the church understood itself *in communion:* as a community, not just a hierarchy, united as members of Christ's body by their baptism. As the council documents declare over and over, the church is the *people of God* who, regardless of their status in the church, take part in the mission and ministry to which Christ calls us. This community of the church announces the coming of God's kingdom, which is both "at hand" and awaiting us at the end of time, as Jesus proclaimed it (Mk 1:15; Mt 24:29–31). The kingdom may not be fully realized in our church or in our world now—but we can't wait till the hereafter to attain it. We lean into it, and in a sense *live* into it, so that "kingdom come" becomes the *kingdom coming,* arriving within us in every hour. This is a tall order for the people of God; but as the saying goes, somebody's got to do it, and that somebody is the church.

The church as community also sees itself in communion with people of other Christian denominations and other faiths—all those who seek the face of God and the goodness of their sisters and brothers. So we can see that this model of church doesn't intend to establish a little utopian community for its own sake; the church community exists for the sake of the whole world, to draw all to the light of Christ and the goodness of God.

How does it seek to do all that? As any counselor is quick to say, we can't change others; we can only change ourselves. So the church community focuses on becoming a better witness to the kingdom of God so that its testimony is credible to the outside world. First and foremost, the church does that through inspiring and formative worship in the Sunday assembly. Ritual has always held great power in people's lives—consider what saluting the American flag meant to us after the events of September 11, 2001, or what the rituals of birthdays and Christmases meant for you as a child, every time enacted in the same memorable and unalterable sequence. For Catholics the liturgy has great power to inform, re-form, and transform our minds and hearts and establish a profound sense of identity and purpose. Celebrated well, liturgy can build up faith and challenge us to become what we profess. It is also true that poor liturgy—halfheartedly led, faintly preached, and badly sung—can damage faith, sometimes severely.

Herein lies the problem with the community model of church. A vital community is obviously desirable and beneficial, but in order to participate in such a society, you have to *find* it. So much depends on factors outside of your control: local leadership and its talents or experience; the character of the assembly; the resources of the community, which shape the environment and possibly limit the music program. Add to those factors the limitations of your own willingness and availability to work toward changing what feels unacceptable. The community model of church is a tenuous one to hang your hat on, because even the ideal community can change overnight with the arrival of a new pastor or the loss of certain key resources. Some who become alienated from the church do so because they can't find the community they are looking for or because they had it but lost it. It is important to remember that this sense of the perfect community is subjective. When the Latin Mass was replaced with the vernacular version, many responded with dismay and even horror. The dignified, silent, private worship they cherished seemed banished in an hour, replaced with folk guitars and hand shaking and an artificial atmosphere of friendly cheer. Others met the "new Mass" with a sigh of relief and gratitude: at last, here was a communal worship that spoke to their hearts!

The sense of church as community is crucial, but like the other aspects of church, it is unwise to put all your eggs in this one notoriously fragile basket. There can never be a community that suits everyone just right, and the one that meets our needs right now may seem very inadequate at another phase in our spiritual journey.

THE CHURCH AS SERVANT: DOING AS JESUS DID

"Going to Mass and receiving the sacraments and saying your prayers is all very well and good," Rob says. "But it doesn't mean a thing if you don't live it." He is absolutely firm on this point. "Personal piety and getting your moral act together can make you a better person, I suppose. But does it feed the hungry? Does it visit the sick and imprisoned? Does it bring good news to the poor? Those are the things that Jesus asked us to do, and if we don't do those, we've got nothing to show for ourselves!"

Rob has introduced the sticking point for many who view Christianity from the outside and find it wanting. The matter of integrity or hypocrisy is crucial in the realm of faith. Are we who we say we are? Is our faith real or a show? Rob insists that real Christians are known by their love and that love is demonstrated by one's service to others. After all, that's how Jesus did it, and he's our Lord.

It is useful to look at the multiple models of the church in terms of who gets served by each. The institutional model exists to serve its membership. The mystical union model serves the genuine seeker. The herald model serves the messenger who bears the word and the world that is invited to embrace it. The community model serves those who participate in it, with an eye to witnessing to the greater society. In this light, it is fair to say that the servant model of church offers something unique and significant to the picture of what church means. For the servant model is at the service of the poor.

Who could argue with this key understanding of church? We cannot follow Jesus more closely than when we imitate his example. When the church serves, ministering to the poor, the sick, the rejected, or the outcast, and works to bring about justice and peace for the least of our sisters and brothers, it most clearly resembles the Lord we are following. Generosity, compassion, and self-sacrifice are at the heart of what it means to be Christian. Although Catholicism has no monopoly on helping those in need, it has proved to be particularly good at it. The history of the church overflows with stories of people—some famous saints, many others quiet and ordinary—who have devoted themselves to serving others. With the example of Jesus to guide them, folks like St. Francis of Assisi laid down all worldly benefits for the sake of embracing Christ in the poor. St. Camillus de Lellis took on the ministry of those who were sick and were too marginalized to gain access to medical care. St. Katharine Drexel opened the doors to education and opportunity in the United States for children of color. Catherine McAuley worked with destitute women on the streets of Ireland. Catherine de Hueck Doherty founded Friendship House to facilitate dialogue and community in the midst of racial division. St. Maximilian Kolbe, a priest, accepted martyrdom in place of another man at Auschwitz. Dorothy Day insisted that service to the poor was about justice, not mere charity. In our own day folks like Mother Teresa lifted the dignity of the dying in India; César Chávez and Dolores Huerta brought the plight of the migrant farmworker to the nation's attention; and Philip Berrigan led his family and friends in a lifetime protest regarding the notion of war itself, serving years in prison for the urgent cause of peace.

This too is the church, illustrated to us in the heroism of a few but supported by the less visible daily sacrifices of many for the cause of the voiceless and the hopeless. In Catholic hospitals, schools, social service agencies, shelters, soup kitchens, and foreign missions, the poor Christ is welcomed and served. For those who encounter human kindness at the local Catholic Charities agency, who are clothed, fed, and sheltered at Catholic Worker houses of hospitality in many cities, or who are served as refugees by Catholic Relief Services worldwide, this face of the church is one that is most readily understood and urgently sought.

Where do such heroic impulses and generous hands come from? From the church's tradition (courtesy of the institution); from its communion with the generous love of God (with its source in the gracious mystery); from its attention to the word of God made flesh in Jesus (thanks to the herald); and from the lived encounter with sisters and brothers who seek to take this journey of faith together in joyous and responsive worship (our church community). In all these ways, the sons and daughters of the church are inspired to demonstrate their concern for those who lack the basic physical and spiritual necessities of life and to give of themselves—even sacrificially—to bring some relief to the suffering of the human family. These ordinary heroes follow the lead of a church that speaks up for the oppressed, the defenseless, those on the margins, those whom the powerful would rather ignore. Arguably, the world would be a considerably more painful place without the works of mercy Catholics have performed throughout the ages and the call to justice that challenges the mighty on their thrones to consider whose law they are overriding with their own. The servant tradition of concern and advocacy for the needy calls us all to show this same compassion and sense of justice in our dealings with family, friends, coworkers, strangers, and other members of society.

Very, very few people who feel compelled to leave the church cite the service role of the church as the reason for their departure. More often those who leave the institutional church remain "Catholic" in their responsiveness to the poor and their keen sense of justice for the afflicted. In fact, some justice workers focus so much of their life's energy on the cause of alleviating human suffering that their departure from organized religion, worship, and creed is almost incidental to their increased outpouring of Christian service.

THE QUESTION REVISITED

We began this chapter with a direct question: what do you want from the church? And we have presented a fivefold model for formulating an answer to that important inquiry. First, you might consider from which aspects of the church you feel alienated: from the institution, from union with God, from the gospel message, from the worshiping assembly of faith, or from the role of servant. Once you arrive at that answer, you might also ask yourself which aspects of these five facets of church are most meaningful to you and most painful to lose.

Most Catholics, even the lifelong, faithful, practicing kind, would admit that certain aspects of the fivefold meaning of church are less important to them than others. Some aspects may be compelling and bring life; others are tangential and less relevant. There may be churchgoing Catholics out there who never bump heads with the institution, are at peace with God, embrace the gospel and the community, and offer their service without experiencing any conflict all around. Good for them—but chances are you're not one of them. So maybe the goal is to consider whether any of these models of church are compelling enough to keep you within, or even at the margins of, church membership. Do you want this church, any of it, and how willing are you to work with the sources of disharmony (even as they seem to work against you) in order to hold on to what's vital to your faith?

For many Catholics, accepting an imperfect church locked within a particular hour of human history is a doable proposition. Perhaps some are motivated by the vision of what the church *might* be, seeing their role as almost prophetic within it—in a sense, playing herald to the herald. Others are just as adamant in their desire to work hard to change the church—being a servant to the servant. Some may just want to find a quiet corner away from all the politics of church to work on their spirituality, and the mystery aspect of church embraces that person too. But certainly, whatever kind of Catholic one is, a relationship with all five models of church is unavoidable. Catholics who make their peace with the church find room for all five, even if détente is the best they can do with some of them. This is a lot to think about. You may want to take some time to reflect on what the church really means to you before you head on to the next chapter.

FIVE

What Does It Take to Be Catholic?

A friend tells the story about the time he attended a priest's first Mass. (This event, usually celebrated soon after the priest's ordination, can be a little like a wedding in one sense: lots of family and friends attend, some of whom have not been inside a church in a long time and some of whom have never been in a Catholic church at all.) When the newly ordained priest stood up to deliver his homily, he looked out over the assembled guests and said, "Here we are, gathered together, and the roof has not fallen down." He acknowledged what some were undoubtedly thinking. He also made an acute observation about the community of faith: that a group of individuals, with a variety of relationships to the church, some good, some not so good, can gather together in common celebration without fear. This reality not only shows that the church can withstand such a conglomeration but acknowledges that, in fact, this is precisely what the church looks like.

Catholicism is often misperceived from the outside as a universal organism caught up in a papal "mind meld." Nothing could be further from the truth; the church's unity should never be mistaken for mere uniformity. The word *catholic* means "universal"—reflecting a common purpose and outlook rooted in our oneness in Christ. The Catholic Church, then, is more like a big tent than a colony of clones. The "big tent" vision is one the church has embraced since the time of the apostles: Jews and Gentiles, men and women, the enslaved and the free all have a place here (Gal 3:28). In its assembly the church gathers up saints and sinners, the devout and the doubtful, the pious, the irreverent, and everyone in between who has chosen to travel this journey together. It's not a perfect system, and it's not for perfect people. As another priest once said in a stirring call to communion, "Let the sinners here present come forward to receive the life of Christ, which is poured out for the sake of forgiveness. Those who have not sinned can all go home." Needless to say, not a soul in the place moved toward the door.

Knowing we are all united in the mercy of Christ is not the same as feeling welcome in the arms of the church, however. As we saw in the last chapter, church can mean many things. Just as we may feel alienated from one or more aspects of our Catholic identity, so we also seek confirmation that we are accepted and acceptable in more ways than one. What does the church expect from those who would share the name Catholic? Another way of asking the same question is: What does it take to be a Catholic?

In this chapter we'll look at some key elements that make up Catholic identity. These are the very things that may get broken when a person becomes alienated from the church. Specifically, we'll be looking at our relationship to the Eucharist, to Catholic moral teaching, to the practice of confession, to the church's ideals concerning marriage, to social justice, and to the overall mission of the church. To make peace with the church—for the sake of returning or of moving beyond bitterness—it is helpful to examine where the fabric of the relationship has been torn.

For some alienated Catholics, leaving the church was not really a decision that was made but rather a gradual drifting away from a practice that was not clearly focused to begin with or had lost its meaning as a result of difficult events. If leaving the church was never really chosen but more a byproduct of circumstances, how do you define "coming back"? What does being an "active" Catholic mean, and what do you have to do to consider yourself one? Exploring the following elements of Catholic identity may answer those questions for you. Since there are many doors through which one "exits" the church, there are several return routes available as well.

DRAW CLOSER TO THE EUCHARIST

If you asked just about anyone on the planet what it means to be Catholic, the most likely response would reflect the one thing Catholics do most publicly: go to Mass. Every Hollywood movie that includes a Catholic character is bound, sooner or later, to show a scene in the middle of an assembly with a fully vested priest up front and a whole lot of ritual going on. It is a stereotype for a good reason: the Eucharist is the center of the Catholic Christian's life.

Yet it is also true that lots of Catholics have a conflicted relationship with the Mass, and many who fall out of relationship with the church cite Mass attendance as one of the reasons. If the Mass is essential to Catholic identity, it's actually a good thing that people take it seriously enough to wrestle with it, demand something from it, and sometimes find it wanting. In other words, if you expect to "get something out of Mass," you are not being selfish or unreasonable. What we get from our participation in the liturgy varies from Mass to Mass, but we are right to look for *something* with which to build up our faith.

Consider what Catholics believe about the Mass: that Christ is really present in the assembly gathered in his name, in the person of the presiding priest, in the Scripture proclaimed, and in consecrated bread and wine through which we actually join ourselves to the body and blood of Jesus in communion. Those are enormous claims. If they were true, wouldn't you choose to participate in that event? If Christ is truly present in our midst and invites us to share in his life, on a visceral flesh-and-blood level, isn't that just plain miraculous? And wouldn't our whole outlook be transformed by the infusion of Christ's life into our being? What would life be like if we took this crucial aspect of faith to heart and lived out of the identity of being Christ for others in our caring, forgiving, serving, and celebrating?

Catholics extend this belief about the centrality of the Eucharist to the adoration of the Blessed Sacrament and prayers before the tabernacle, which can be profound experiences of the presence of God, who is always in our midst. And everything from crucifixes to statues to images of the Sacred Heart displayed in homes speaks of the Catholic insistence on the spiritual and tangible presence of Christ in our lives. Even our prayers for the intercession of the saints demonstrate the Catholic idea that religious experience is always *mediated*—that is, it's a spiritual reality made known to us through some tangible medium. One of the great Catholic understandings is that pure spirituality is not available to finite humans caught within the limitations of time and place. If we are to know God, who is pure spirit, we must know God through the medium of the *Incarnation,* God made flesh. Jesus is our primary and most perfect mediator, and through him we learn how all of creation speaks God's name to us. As Jesuit poet Gerard Manley Hopkins says in "God's Grandeur": "The world is charged with the grandeur of God." Our experience of Christ in the bread and wine of the Eucharist teaches us how the sacred dwells implicitly in every ordinary thing.

Once we come to that crucial understanding—that common things hold sacred realities—we can follow the Catholic Christian vision everywhere and in all things. Once we see Jesus in the Eucharist, in the meal, in Scripture, in the priest, in the assembly, our gaze moves outward. We begin to recognize him in the least and the last, in the disadvantaged, the sick, the strangers and outcasts, the prisoners, the enemy—all those folks who might normally be excluded. When we acknowledge and claim Christ in all of these ways, we begin to see the value of human life as God does. And we come to see that no life is expendable.

The eucharistic vision is a critical way of perceiving reality for people of faith. We can see how the belief that creation is infused with God's life leads to a clearer understanding of every other church teaching: the right to life of the unborn, the rejection of capital punishment, the call to justice for the poor, the embrace of nonviolent ways and means. It is no wonder that drawing close to the Eucharist is the shortest route to being "in communion" with the Catholic way of life. The longer we meditate on its meaning, the deeper our understanding of "the way, the truth, and the life" that Jesus invited us to share when he said, "Take and eat: this is my body."

Fidelity to the Eucharist, whether as a daily practice or within the Sunday gathering, is one way we reinforce the memory of this vision and remain faithful to it in our relationships and responsibilities. Is the Eucharist a magic formula that provides us with hidden strength and wisdom? Will it fill us with grace in some automatic sense—we show up, and grace gets dumped into us by the bucketful? No, of course not. Yet through our faithful presence—sometimes mindful, sometimes idle—we acclimate ourselves to the possibility of transformation of our minds, our hearts, our eyes, and our days. "Do this in memory of me," Jesus says to us again and again through the action of the Mass. Learning to live what we "remember" is the work of a lifetime. Every act of love we practice deepens our hearts to receive the next.

It is useful to note that the word *Eucharist* means "thanksgiving." Our fidelity to this ritual is ultimately an expression of our gratitude to God for all that we have and are. If we choose to be a eucharistic people, we are choosing a life of gratefulness, willing to forgive as we are forgiven, capable of compassion because of God's great mercy shown to us, open to love because love is our source and our destination in God.

If you have been separated from the church and have refrained from joining in this celebration of gratitude, perhaps the most significant way to claim your place in the church is to take your seat at the table of the Lord once more. There are plenty of reasons that you might have felt it necessary to stay away and only one reason to return: because Jesus himself has invited us to be here.

MAKE INFORMED, MORAL DECISIONS

All too often morality gets boiled down to the business of sexual decision making. This is terribly unfortunate because being a moral person is so much broader than that. In fact, we should just say that being a *person* is so much larger than that. What we do with our time, our money, our talent, and our relationships across the board is at least as important as what decisions we make in the use of our sexuality. Yet even in Jesus' time, a lot of people seemed very happy to equate sin with sexual lawbreaking and to ignore the laws of mercy, charity, justice, and giving to God what is God's.

In this respect, the church's moral teachings have been wonderfully broad and dynamic, but regretfully, more attention has been paid to promoting sexual mores than any other kind. Many people who feel compelled to leave the church, as opposed to drifting away from it, do so because they do not think they can accept or live up to what the church has to say about sex. So after admitting that a lot of church leaders and teachers have overidentified morality with toeing the line sexually, we'd like to look at what the church's moral teachings really have to say.

A cornerstone of Catholic teaching is that the informed personal conscience is the highest authority to which each of us has to answer. No one, not even the church, has the right to compel us to act against our conscience. This is not the same as saying we can do anything we want or anything "we can live with." The key word on which this teaching hinges is *informed*. Following an ignorant conscience is no better than taking advice from a known fool. We have an obligation to follow our conscience, which includes a more primary responsibility to educate our conscience in order to be able to *discern* the direction of our lives. Discernment is more than making a decision, more than adding up the pros and cons and choosing the one that best suits our intentions. Discernment involves choosing a path based on wisdom and truth. Christian discernment is how we clarify what God's best hopes for our lives might be, according to the teachings of Jesus, in every moment of decision.

So how do we inform our consciences in order to have proper discernment? We are not left in the dark in this matter of great importance. First, we have the word of God in Scripture as well as the signs of the sacraments, which direct our lives to the holy work of welcoming, healing, forgiving, loving, sharing, thanking, and serving. The Christian community is also available to us for support, encouragement, and the good examples demonstrated by the saints. In addition to that, we have the ongoing body of the church's teachings. If you went to Catholic school or CCD classes or modern religious education programs in the parish, you probably are familiar with the basic moral teachings—the Ten Commandments of the Old Testament, the Beatitudes of the New Testament, the corporal and spiritual works of mercy—if you were awake long enough to hear them taught. As any schoolteacher will tell you, the problem with education is that it's wasted on kids. Adults are the ones who really need to hear this stuff!

But knowing how to acquire an informed conscience is not the same as agreeing on the necessity of having one. One of the obstacles many people presently face in framing the business of morality is that, frankly, they aren't quite sure that sin is a problem. Christianity's traditional teaching on sin and salvation lacks considerable punch if you remove sin from the equation. Not everyone sees the need to be "saved" or the reason it should make a difference that Jesus "died for our sins." The perceived lack of relevance of this central doctrine of Christianity probably accounts to a significant extent for the alienation of many, especially the young, from organized Christianity as a whole.

Not to address this doubt is to end the conversation before it starts. It is a modern notion to dismiss the concept of sin in favor of life's "mistakes" or "lessons" and to avoid the negative labeling of ourselves as "sinners." Much of this outlook can be seen as healthy. Human beings should not define themselves by their sinfulness or perceive themselves as hopelessly imperiled, without a savior to rescue them from their own worst impulses. The doctrine of original sin, an attempt to express why human beings choose wrong even when they are capable of choosing right, went far south of its meaning when people began to think of their true nature as "original depravity." Our present society has a much more positive attitude toward human nature and its goodness and has recognized the importance of a sense of self-worth for a healthy life and a fundamental respect for others. Many Christian churches, the Catholic Church included, have moved toward emphasizing the "original goodness" of the world that God created: "God looked at everything he had made, and he found it very good" (Gn 1:31 NAB). While bumper stickers abound announcing in one way or another the common agreement that "bad things happen," we are remarkably reluctant to own up to our part and to say, "We do bad things"—much less to see these events as what we mean by human sinfulness.

Largely because of the insights of psychology, we now understand that the source of much of our behavior lies buried in past events and hidden impulses arising from the subconscious. Though this awareness has been a good thing, the downside has been a greater and greater difficulty for many to take personal responsibility for their actions, especially when those actions are hurtful. It's ironic: knowing ourselves better has made us less able to take hold of the reins of our lives.

When the idea of sin loses its relevance, we may also reduce the sense of our vital participation in where our lives are going. The problem may be semantic, so let's seek better language rather than rejecting the insight of religious wisdom outright. Certainly, life as it comes to us is a mixed bag. God created us with a remarkable and perilous freedom, including the capacity to turn from our Creator and harm others, ourselves, and our world. But God also made us with a strong sense of urgency to draw close to the source of love. Christian tradition teaches that we have the desire for what is good because our source is in God's goodness. Because of the habit of wrongdoing, however, we don't attain it. That's where God steps in. Salvation is the way God opens the path of goodness long after we've closed and barricaded it by our own choices. It doesn't mean we never make another bad decision. Rather we learn to acknowledge the damage we do and to seek its transformation through the power of God's grace.

This is the start of moral living: admitting that we fail in our efforts to live rightly and that we need God's help to do better. From there morality is not quite a done deal but a *process*—that terrible word that means we're never really finished but always on the road between here and more. So once we consciously enter into the process of moral formation, we are finally ready to admit we can use all the help we can get.

That's where the church is ready to oblige. As ethicist Timothy E. O'Connell observes in *Principles for a Catholic Morality* (San Francisco: Harper & Row, 1990), living a Catholic moral life includes being open to guidance from others. In *Morality: The Catholic View,* French moral theologian Servais Pinckaers elaborates on this idea:

> Catholic moral teaching is not a mere code of prescriptions and prohibitions. It is not something that the church teaches merely to keep people obedient, doing violence to their freedom. Rather, Catholic morality is a response to the aspirations of the human heart for truth and goodness. As such, it offers guidelines that when followed make these aspirations grow and become strong under the warm light of the gospel. Catholic morality is not by nature oppressive. . . . It seeks to educate for growth. This is its true mission. (Servais Pinckaers, *Morality: The Catholic View* [South Bend, Indiana: St. Augustine's Press, 2003], 1)

Catholic moral teaching, then, is not to be reduced to a mere catalog of crime and punishment. It's not a stick to keep people in line or to separate the true believers from the doubters or an excuse to ride roughshod over people's consciences and best judgments. Of course, it *has* been used in these ways by church leaders. But, as O'Connell writes:

> In the final analysis . . . the wisdom and the judgment of the church are important, but they are not supremely important. Therefore, the genuinely important role of church teaching must never be allowed to deteriorate into a "loyalty test" for Catholics. Is a Catholic who finds himself or herself able to agree with the judgment of the church a better Catholic than one who cannot? We must never say so. For just as to use church teaching properly is to celebrate it, to ask it to be more than it is, is to destroy it. (Timothy E. O'Connell, *Principles for a Catholic Morality* [San Francisco: Harper & Row, 1990], 118)

So Catholic moral life involves recognizing the need to be formed by Christian moral principles by being open to the wisdom of others, including the church's moral teaching. Catholic morality also includes acting in accord with your sense of responsibility and the moral principles to which you are listening.

We have been trying to open a window on the process of moral living to show that living a moral life is more than memorizing lists of rules, like the Ten Commandments, and then trying not to break them. The bottom line on living a moral Christian life grows out of faith in the person of Jesus; that is the starting point. Faith, as Pinckaers points out, is not merely adherence to a creed or a certain opinion about life but a commitment of one person to another. The primary commitment Christians make is to Jesus Christ as we come to know him in Scripture, liturgy, prayer, and the people around us.

In the end, O'Connell says, living a Catholic moral life means more than making a commitment to behave ethically. A Catholic moral life also means having a spiritual life that both nourishes and expresses your moral commitment. It means participating in a worshiping community. Referring to Romans 12–15, Pinckaers says, "The Christian life is true worship. . . . where we offer to God as a living sacrifice our bodies and our persons" (Servais Pinckaers, *Morality: The Catholic View,* South Bend, Indiana: St. Augustine's Press, 2003, 12–13). Moral living is a form of worship. Our lives become a kind of liturgy before God, a sacrifice of praise and an offering of love.

Rightly understood, this exploration of what Catholic morality means hasn't let anybody off the hook. This is an adult discussion of morality; if you feel that it only complicates the matter enormously, you heard it right. Some might prefer a checklist of dos and don'ts by which to measure themselves (and their neighbors). Moral living is a whole lot more challenging than that.

SEEK RECONCILIATION

Second on the list of every Hollywood stereotype of Catholicism is the scene in the confessional. (Never mind that most churches now use a "reconciliation room" rather than the dark booth with the heavy velvet curtain. The booth films better!) Deep in the heart of most Catholics over a certain age lies the memory of being behind that curtain, scarcely breathing, waiting for the screen between them and the priest to slide open and the moment of admission of guilt to begin. The dread of the dark that we had when we were young was coupled with the perceived darkness of our souls, and the overall effect could be nerve-wracking.

The sacrament, then known as "penance" or simply "confession," tended to focus on the negative aspects of the occasion: the listing of one's transgressions and the price to be paid, in works or prayers, to amend one's record. All of this may have fit the style of another era, and it certainly expressed the relationship between sin and human accountability of which it sought to make us mindful. But since the renewal of the church brought on by Vatican II, the sacrament has been reconsidered as the "rite of reconciliation," emphasizing the true goal of the occasion: making our peace with God. The anonymous nature of the old ritual is now optional, replaced with a freedom to own who we are and what we've done with the confidence of those who come not to beg for forgiveness they scarcely expect but to claim the mercy God has already promised us.

The sacrament of reconciliation is grounded in the assurance that God's forgiveness is always available and does not have to be earned. In fact, we cannot deserve it. There is nothing we can do to merit what God offers and Jesus so poignantly demonstrates in the outpouring of love on the cross. We do not go to confession to be forgiven by the priest or to have God's forgiveness dispensed by a third party. The rite of forgiveness is given to us because sin is a matter that concerns the whole church. No one commits wrong in isolation. When we choose against love, it affects us and our primary relationships and ultimately our relationship with the God of love. Sometimes, in circumstances of grave sin, our actions may cause harm to the wider community as well. Since the effect of wrongdoing is not private, our reconciliation must also be acknowledged publicly by the church, whose witness is the priest. As with all sacraments, the ritual offers concrete assurance that the God we cannot see is with us and the grace we cannot touch reaches out to redeem us. This word *redeem* means essentially "to buy back"—to get us out of hock, where sin has abandoned us like a treasure in a pawnshop. God does not intend to let a treasured life lay hidden and forfeit. To say that God saves us is simply to say that love will find a way.

If *sin* describes our capacity to do harm and *salvation* means the remedy for sin, then *forgiveness* refers to one of the ways salvation becomes real in our lives. Many of us would agree that forgiveness mends the tears in human relationships. But fewer may connect the forgiveness we offer each other with the forgiveness God always extends to human beings. In Christianity the connection is clear: "Forgive, and you will be forgiven," Jesus says (Lk 6:37 NRSV). That things go wrong is not the end; we are not condemned to live in the wreckage of our mistakes. God understands how the world works, and God has made available a way to make right our wronged relationships, to get them going once again in a wholesome direction. The Hebrew root for the word *forgiveness* means "to be covered." God's forgiveness means that, no matter how badly we fail the mandate to love, God has us covered.

God's forgiveness is guaranteed; but to make peace between each other and within ourselves requires something more. This is the starting point of reconciliation. The process of reconciliation begins with the acknowledgment that we all make choices, sometimes really terrible ones, for less than loving reasons—and live to regret them and desire to make amends. The Catholic rite of reconciliation provides us with four steps to take when sin abounds and we had a starring role to play. First, we are asked to contemplate the wrong, name it and own our part in it, and admit to the damage we caused. Next we express our sorrow for what we have done or failed to do (we make a genuine act of contrition). Third, we accept the consequences of wrongdoing and agree to do what we can to make the situation right (we agree to make restitution). Finally, we resolve to try to avoid the mistake in the future (we firmly commit to amend our lives). Sometimes we can't take back a hurt or undo the damage; that's when God's power to heal and make whole becomes necessary and an act of faith in God is required of us. From the perspective of faith, the story of the human race can be summed up in four words: We sin; God saves. It would be a gross miscalculation of pride to imagine that we can devise a wrong too great for God to make right.

If you feel alienated from the church for things you have done, or things you failed to do, and you believe you need reconciliation, nothing stands between you and the reception of the sacrament. Priests often tell the story of how even non-Catholics occasionally find their way into the confessional, feeling the need to unburden themselves and recognizing no other place where sin can be named openly, sorrow expressed, and amendment sought. As a baptized member of the church, you have a right to this sacrament and its sure route to healing and peace.

APPROACH MARRIAGE SACRAMENTALLY

A wedding is one of the happiest occasions in the lives of those who love. It often involves one of the largest and most expensive celebrations of a lifetime, complete with special costume, ornate environment, formal roles for many participants, photographs, flowers, music, food—the works. The event can take a year to plan; reservations are made at the church and the hall to secure the date, and invitations are sent out months in advance. If all the time, money, and effort that go into planning a wedding is any indication, the marriage of two people is a very serious business. And yet, as we know, marriages can falter and fail. What was supposed to last a lifetime can come apart overnight. No human institution, marriage included, can promise success and permanence. We mortals can say "forever," but the best we can do is offer our intentions.

Generations of Catholics have been separated from their church through the specter of a broken marriage. It was insult added to injury: the heartbreak of a crucial relationship shattered was too often met with silence, if not outright accusation, on the part of church officials. Spouses in abusive situations were counseled to remain in them for the sake of the sacrament or the children. Spouses in loveless unions were told it was their responsibility to lie in the bed they had made for themselves. When those spouses determined that enough was enough, they were told that the consequence of their divorce was a kind of sacramental "divorce" as well: they were no longer welcome to receive Holy Communion. What a grave injustice and sorrow to visit on already hurting people! It was a horrible miscalculation of pastoral action: to "protect" the sacrament at the expense of the people for whom it was intended.

How did we ever get to this point? The trouble centered in the official Catholic definition of marriage—which implies that the solution would have to be found by revisiting that definition. For many years both church and society viewed marriage legalistically as a *contract,* with its primary purpose the procreation and education of children. In other words, marrying couples consented to a contractual relationship for the sake of creating families. As family stability was jeopardized by divorce, it was the responsibility of the couple to keep things together despite whatever private agony that entailed. (Little attention was given to the fact that families in agony likewise imperil the fate of children.)

Since 1983, with the publication of a revised version of canon law (the law of the church), the church's official view of marriage has shifted from characterizing marriage as a contract to regarding it as a *covenant,* or promise. In this more biblical understanding, a woman and a man establish a partnership of total self-giving to each other for the rest of their lives. The purpose of this covenant is not only having and raising children but also what the church calls the "good of the spouses"—the wife and husband living for the good of the other and thus for the marriage. This definition acknowledges that the *partnership* of the couple is one of the natural "ends" of marriage. Therefore a fruitful marriage is defined not only by the presence of children but also by the love that nourishes and sustains two people. Without that, the Catholic conditions of a sacramental marriage are not genuinely met.

Much less legalistic than a contract, a covenant evokes the spiritual nature of marriage. *Covenant* is the same word used to describe the relationship between God and the people of God in the Bible. God's love for us serves as a model for the marriage relationship. Just as God's love is faithful, life-giving, and without end, so is the love between spouses. A marriage grows with its roots in fidelity, fruitfulness, and permanence, and the church sees these elements as essential for the union.

The church believes that when two people marry, certain other conditions need to be in place for the marriage to be valid and complete. Both parties must be in a situation to make a good judgment about the important decision they are making. They must be reasonably free of serious emotional or psychological problems (which, again, would hinder their ability to discern their choice). They need to believe in marriage as the church understands it, and they must be willing to commit to each other for life, to be faithful, to be open to children, and to care for each other. In addition, they cannot enter into marriage out of fear, under force, or because of deception, and they must have a reasonable understanding of what marriage entails and whom they are marrying. Finally, they cannot place any conditions on the other person.

The Catholic Church expects baptized Catholics to marry "in the church"; that is, to seek the sacrament of marriage rather than only a civil union. Getting married in the church includes fulfilling the premarital process your particular diocese recommends as well as exchanging vows and celebrating the wedding in a Catholic church before a priest or deacon and at least two witnesses.

Despite all the concerns the church may raise before two people receive the sacrament, a significant percentage of marriages do not work out. Some couples will fake their way through the prenuptial preparation in order to be married, even though their union does not fulfill the conditions outlined above. They may not be interested in a union that is a reminder of God's covenantal love of humanity, or they may be deceived about their partner's true intentions regarding the commitment. Some just want a church wedding to satisfy their parents. But others do intend to comply with all the images that the church offers about marriage and, as life unfolds, find themselves unable to do so for entirely unforeseeable reasons. For all of these reasons, the church facilitates a process of annulment for those whose marriages are deemed irretrievably lost.

The best way to explain the annulment process is to say that it is a search for understanding, healing, and reconciliation in the delicate circumstance of personal loss and relational failure. Annulment seeks to uncover what a marriage *lacked,* what key aspect of the covenant was missing for a marriage to be sacramentally valid. Because the church first teaches that marriage is indissoluble and then offers the possibility of annulment, this process is one of the most misunderstood areas of Catholic practice. Bad information abounds, some of it from church officials themselves and some from well-meaning Catholic friends and relatives. Some will say that Catholics who marry outside the church, or get divorced and remarry outside the church, are automatically excommunicated—that is, banned from participation in the sacraments. Others may believe the church considers the children of an annulled marriage to be illegitimate. Or that an annulment is really just a "Catholic divorce." Or that the annulment process places the blame on or excludes the other spouse, or focuses too much on the beginning of the failed marriage, or is really just for young people who want to get remarried. Cynics will even tell you that annulments are only granted to those rich enough to buy one.

None of the above is true. But that's not to say the process can't be difficult, painful, time consuming, and puzzling. Any circumstance that obliges us to return to the scene of our failures in love is not going to be particularly pleasant. But coming to terms with the past and making peace with our failures is an extension of the work of reconciliation that the church embodies. Reconciling ourselves with the past makes us free to enter the future and its opportunities for loving relationships of many kinds, with an open heart.

An annulment is granted when a church tribunal determines a marriage to be invalid because it lacks one of the conditions of sacramental union outlined previously. Folks often say that an annulment means the marriage "never happened," but that way of looking at the situation is misleading. Yes, an annulment does take the marriage "off the books" as a sacrament. Neither of the ex-spouses is bound to the marriage any longer, and they are unmarried in the eyes of the church, free to approach the sacrament of matrimony in the future. But an annulment does not say the couple didn't love each other or didn't have a marriage in other ways. It does not dismiss the legal and lawful components of civil marriage (which is why the church requires a civil divorce before an annulment can be sought). An annulment simply says the marriage was not *complete* according to the Catholic understanding of what a marriage is. It lacked something crucial from the beginning, something that the couple never found and that proved fatal to their union in the end.

Annulments can be expensive, but most dioceses accept payment on a sliding scale and offer free service to those who need it; absence of money will never hold up the process. Also, most people who work in diocesan marriage tribunals work hard, with great integrity, and are not susceptible to pressure and favor seeking, despite what some pastors believe.

Despite all the church does to prepare its members for sacramental marriage and to assist them in acquiring an annulment if the union fails, some still question why it's the church's business at all when a marriage ends. The church claims the right to decide the validity of marriage because it also believes that when baptized people marry—Catholic or not—their marriage becomes sacramentally binding (which is why a civil divorce cannot, in the eyes of the church, end a marriage). Even though nothing short of death can end a valid sacramental union, the church is realistic and acknowledges that marriages do end, and for quite specific reasons that it is in our best interest to come to terms with.

If you feel the need to explore your particular situation— whether married civilly, divorced, remarried, or contemplating marriage—it is best to talk with an informed and compassionate member of a parish staff: a priest, deacon, or pastoral associate. (If you had this conversation once before and it has been some years, you might find that you receive a better reception at this time or in another parish.) If you don't know of a person to contact, ask someone you trust for a referral or call the chancery of your diocese and ask to speak to someone about an annulment. And if you are not satisfied with the first church representative you talk with, feel free to get another opinion. Your marriage situation is very important to you *and* to the church, but it should not be an impediment to your life within the community of faith.

EMBRACE THE WORLD COMMUNITY

So far we've looked at Catholic identity from the perspective of the eucharistic gathering, moral living, the practice of reconciliation, and marriage. All of these aspects of our lives fit into a wider scheme of things in the society around us. As a professor once replied to a student inquiring whether his course was about personal ethics or social ethics, "What would a *personal* ethic possibly be?" Catholics do not live in a ghetto of private beliefs; we hold convictions about the meaning of our humanity as a whole.

Catholic social teaching deals with the church's vision of how society should work for the benefit of the human person. It is grounded in the belief that God is the source and destination of all that is. The book of Genesis describes the event of creation in this way: "Then God said, 'Let us make humankind in our image, according to our likeness.' . . . So God created humankind in his image, in the image of God he created them; male and female he created them" (Gn 1:26–27 NRSV). Humanity bears the likeness of God and contains in some measure God's holiness. Out of this sense of the sacredness of all life flow the principles of Catholic social teaching. While it would be difficult to include centuries of thought here, a brief summary may catch the spirit in principle:

Respect for human life. If the gift of life is a sacred trust, then we are stewards and not owners of it. Human life is precious and inviolable—not to be violated—and it is always wrong to attack or jeopardize human persons at any point along the spectrum of life from conception to death. The Catholic respect for life encompasses opposition to war (under any but the most limited terms), to the proliferation of arms, to systems that cause and exploit poverty, as well as to racism, abortion, capital punishment, assisted suicide, and euthanasia—what the late Cardinal Joseph Bernardin described as forces that tear at the "seamless garment of life."

The dignity and rights of people. This sacredness of the human person has a number of important implications. First, regardless of race, gender, age, national origin, religion, sexual orientation, employment or economic status, intelligence, level of achievement in life, health, or any other factor, every person has dignity. It's not what people do or have done that matters most; it's that God granted them the fullness of life, which cannot be denied. Second, human dignity gives us a claim to belong to a community, the human family, which safeguards our rights, including the right to practice our faith.

Special protection of the poor, vulnerable, and afflicted. Social activist Dorothy Day, now a candidate for sainthood, cofounded the Catholic Worker Movement to give voice to the plight of the homeless and to bring relief to their suffering. She fed, sheltered, and fought for the poor because she took chapter 25 of the Gospel of Matthew literally. When we feed the hungry, give drink to the thirsty, welcome the stranger, clothe the naked, care for the sick, and visit prisoners (performing some of the corporal works of mercy according to Catholic moral tradition), we do the same for Jesus.

Day, a convert to Catholicism, did not devote her life to following these commandments because she was a do-gooder. She understood that to ignore the suffering of the disadvantaged is to ignore Jesus present in them. Day's witness illustrates a key principle of Catholic social teaching: *all people* have a right to life, food, shelter, rest, health care, education, and employment. And as Pope John

Paul II continually reminds the church, we have a "preferential option" for the sake of the poor. They make the most urgent claim on the community because their need is the greatest. Society must be judged by how it treats its most vulnerable members and how it forms public policy in regard to them.

Stewardship. While human life holds a special place within creation, all of creation has its source in God and is therefore holy and deserving of respect. Humanity plays a unique role, not as property owners (because creation belongs to God alone) but as "managers" of the earth. God calls us to protect and use our natural environment—land, air, water, and wildlife—responsibly. Stewardship of creation also governs how we employ our individual talents, care for our health, and use our personal resources.

Life together. We find our fulfillment in being with others: within family, as friends, in organizations, and through other voluntary associations. We also realize our dignity and rights in relationship to others. Unrestrained individualism and selfishness can destroy personal relationships as well as those within and between neighborhoods, cities, and nations.

We need community; we also have a right to participate in the shaping of the society in which we live and move and have our being. We want to share in the decisions that affect our lives, especially when it comes to our labor. We have a right to decent and productive work, fair wages with which we can support ourselves and those who depend on us, property ownership, and the freedom to organize. Catholic social teaching also recommends that decision making and problem solving connected to social and political issues be done by those affected and be handled as locally as possible.

Living the principles of Catholic social teaching may seem like a distant orbit in our relationship to the church, but it is really close to the heart of the matter of engaging our faith. We may piously practice the rituals of the church, but until we move outward to our neighbor, we are missing the fullest expression of Christianity. Once, when Jesus was asked what the greatest commandment was, his answer was to love God and love your neighbor as yourself (Mt 22:36–39). The two loves are aspects of the one commandment. We cannot pretend to love God if we dismiss our neighbor out of hand.

Even if other parts of your relationship to the church are not in the greatest shape, by putting these social principles into practice in your life, you enter into and maintain communion with Jesus Christ and the church. If you donate to organizations that provide food relief or if you work directly to feed people (for example, by volunteering at a food pantry or serving meals to the homeless and poor), you are exercising your Catholic faith. If you provide care to an ailing loved one or volunteer at a hospital, you're living the social teachings of the church. If you respect all people you encounter regardless of the differences between them and you; if you refuse to exclude others from groups to which they have a right to belong; if you welcome outsiders, like a lonely neighbor or a child or adolescent or coworker who doesn't fit in; or if you go to the county jail once a month to help lead a Bible study group, you are expressing your faith at the deepest level. Finally, if you begin to think about and take responsibility for your habits of consumption—knowing that what you buy and where it comes from have consequences for the rest of the world—you are exercising your role as a steward of creation.

A vital acceptance of the church's social teachings often enlivens our response to the rituals of worship, as we gain insights into our oneness with others in Christ. For those who find the church unapproachable on Sunday morning, the encounter with your neighbor on Monday through Saturday may be the most sensible place to begin.

EMBRACE THE CHURCH'S MISSION

Mission is a loaded word. On the one hand, we've got the image presented in spy thrillers: the impossible task presented to a hero who must save civilization as we know it. On the other hand, we think of a grass hut in some Third-World country, where robed religious figures are bringing rice and medicine to some struggling and forgotten people. It might be surprising to consider that the church means both of these things in its sense of mission—and much more.

Where did the church's understanding of its mission come from? After the Resurrection, Jesus appeared to his followers and said to them, "Go therefore and make disciples of all nations, baptizing them in the name of the Father and of the Son and of the Holy Spirit" (Mt 28:19 NRSV). The church has drawn from these words its mandate to spread the gospel far and wide. From the beginning of its history, a fundamental part of the church's mission has been to reach new members, and its rapid growth from its roots in Jerusalem to the Near East, throughout the ancient Roman world, and eventually to every continent attests to the missionary emphasis of the church. Even today the church continues to spread the Good News it has been given, to the point that Christianity soon will have more members in Africa, southern Asia, and South America than in Europe and North America.

As significant as the foreign missions are, the church understands its call to mission much more intimately. Each baptized member of the church can be a missionary without the long-distance travel. Vatican II identified the church as a missionary church and its people as a missionary people. Our common mission is the same as when Jesus first announced it to his earliest disciples. At the beginning of his public ministry, Jesus declared in his hometown that God had anointed him to bring good news to the poor, to proclaim liberty to captives and recovery of sight to the blind, and to let the oppressed go free (Lk 4:18). All who are baptized in Christ imitate Jesus' mission, not only to folks far away but to those all around us.

Mission expert Father Anthony Gittins writes that mission "is a job description of God" and that "what God does is move, reach out, embrace, spread goodness, encounter, share" ("Mission: What's It Got To Do with Me?" *The Living Light,* 34 [Spring 1998]: 6–13). Jesus, sent by God and making real God's will on earth, extended this task to all who would follow him. This work is about embracing, including, reconciling, revitalizing, bringing hope, and restoring: this is essentially who God is, as revealed in the life of Jesus. The formal name of bringing God's good news to others is *evangelization.* And we can participate in this evangelizing work in many ways: witnessing to God's love by our love; being a presence of forgiveness and reconciliation; advocating for justice; engaging in dialogue with others who are different from us, which requires our respect and openness to being changed by them; and responding to the needs of others in liberating ways. Participating in the liberation of others, Gittins says, means "setting people free from whatever binds or enslaves: sin or sickness, demons or addictions."

We are used to identifying evangelists as those people on television who preach a fiery message using "insider" religious language or the folks who stand on a milk crate in the park and shout

Bible verses. So it can seem strange to think of ourselves as potential evangelists. Some of us are really uncomfortable with the idea of talking about our faith in public at all: Aren't religion and politics the two things polite people don't talk about? Isn't it wrong to force our beliefs down other people's throats? We can see from this short look at the church's mission that our goal is not *talking* but *witnessing*, which has more to do with who we are than what we say. When we treat people as God would have them treated, when we speak the truth in every social situation no matter what the cost, we *are* proclaiming the liberating message of Jesus, even if we never speak his name.

This kind of Christian testimony is also a basic part of Catholic identity, and it can bring others in contact with the Gospels more powerfully than if you read them chapter and verse. Jesus didn't just preach and teach as he walked from town to town; he performed signs that backed up what he said. When we offer our lives as testimony to our beliefs, we become the living sign that folks around us might be waiting for.

PUTTING IT ALL TOGETHER

Our point is simple: there are many ways to be Catholic. Or in the metaphor that Jesus used at the Last Supper, "In my Father's house are many rooms" (Jn 14:2 RSV). Each of the elements of Catholic identity we've described in this chapter opens the door to one of those rooms. Enter one room, and you're already in the house.

Catholicism has many doors through which we enter and make the life of the church part of our lives. In this chapter we've mentioned some of the more important ones: the sacraments, morality, social teaching, and mission. It may be impossible for you to occupy all these rooms at once; one or two may be enough for now.

For some the institutional church, which maintains the key to the sacramental life of Catholics, may still be too formidable to approach. This does not have to be a deterrent to claiming the other aspects of Catholic Christian life and mission that are ours by virtue of our baptism.

For those who are contemplating a return to parish life or are even just curious about the idea, the next chapter will talk about ways to find a place in the pews that's right for you.

SIX

The Search for the "Good" Parish

We can learn this much from the Protestants: not everyone will agree on what a good expression of church is. If there were such a thing as a perfect parish, chances are all people of goodwill would have made their way to it by now. The parish experience is composed of many parts, not the least of which is the hour of worship. But there are other factors, like the commitment to being a vital community; opportunities for ongoing religious education and spiritual formation; groups for children, teens, singles, parents, and seniors; social outreach, service, and justice activism—just to name a few. Depending on your stage of life and personal inclinations, you will naturally be looking for a specific kind of parish to meet your needs.

For those of us who grew up thinking of the church as one big expression of uniformity, it can be surprising to encounter the range of experiences that reside under the name Catholic. An elderly woman who had lived her whole life in a small town in Pennsylvania visited her grown daughter in the Southwest. Accustomed to the Northeast style of ethnically defined parishes—one for the Polish, the Italians, or the Irish—the older woman was astonished at the Sunday morning assembly. People of every race showed up, and the songs of many languages were sung. There was a bit of dancing in the procession, and at the time of the prayers of the faithful, those in the assembly called out their petitions for prayer spontaneously. The priest smiled and showed good humor in his relationship to the people, not like the solemn face her pastor back home displayed. Overall this Mass followed the form of every liturgy she'd ever been to, and yet it felt entirely new.

Afterward the daughter nervously inquired what her mother thought of it all. The woman replied at once, "Really different." Then after a moment's silence, she added, "But I like the difference." The daughter breathed for the first time that morning.

Some people who leave the church actually walk out on a particular expression of church they find disagreeable or unsatisfying. Part of being a universal church means being large enough to contain a variety of forms and offerings within one creed. Very often it's not the Catholic Church we are struggling with but the local face of that church at the parish level. That is, after all, our connecting point with the whole institution. Relatively few of us will ever see a pope up close, but we greet the local assembly every Sunday. That encounter may be enough to make or break our commitment to the universal church, so it's something to be taken very seriously.

THE IDEA OF THE PARISH

Some question the viability of the traditional notion of the parish in modern circumstances. The parish has been understood as a geographically determined identity. Parish maps used to show the actual limits of the territory, right down to which side of Main Street belonged to St. Brigid's and which to St. Anthony's. If you lived on those streets, you knew which parish had your member-ship. It was that simple.

When older parishes were conceived, of course, they sought to meet the needs of particular immigrant communities that tended to congregate in culture- or language-based ghettos. St. Rita's was built by Italian-speaking people and St. Stanislaus's for the Polish. Everything about those parishes echoed their country of origin, down to the decorations they favored, the feast days they empha-sized, and the style of their worship. If you fell in love across parish boundaries back then, it could be every bit as alarming to your family as if you were planning to marry outside the church! Those were the days—but those days only remain in rare pockets of the American church today.

These days ethnically defined neighborhoods have largely given way to economically determined ones. And the idea of the parish as a geographical entity has also ceded to the ease of mod-ern transportation, which makes it plausible to go farther to attend a service. Coupled with that factor is the reality that some parishes are closing for lack of funds or merging for the sake of serving larger communities in better facilities. A town that supported seven eth-nic parishes a generation ago may now retain only one or two of those sites, making travel on Sunday mornings a necessity rather than a choice. Also, some people commute long distances to get to work every day and may form a close attachment to the parish near their jobs, where they attend daily Mass. For many reasons, we can see that the geographically defined parish is giving way to the parish of convenience or personal preference.

The 2002 Center for Applied Research in the Apostolate (CARA) Catholic Poll found that 25 percent of practicing Catholics do not attend their territorial parish. Nineteen percent say they have shopped around for a parish before choosing one, citing the quality of preaching as a major factor in their selection. The under-thirty crowd is most likely to church-hop. Of those who commit to a parish, the biggest factor mentioned in staying is the ability to participate in activities outside of Mass. These are positive indications that people are becoming more thoughtful about their commitment, more serious about developing their faith, and interested in more than meeting the Sunday obligation and keeping their place in line toward the Pearly Gates.

STEPS TOWARD REENTRY INTO PARISH LIFE

If you have been estranged from or are struggling with the church at this time, you may have read the past several chapters with an eye to diagnosing the problems you have with the church. The experience of alienation has strong emotional and psychological elements that can breed a generalized sense of injury or aversion. But rarely is "everything" wrong with a relationship gone awry, and our relationship to the church is no exception. If you can identify the specific causes of the conflict, the possibility of treatment, cure, or reconciliation may become available to you. Even if you cannot do much about the particular problems that create obstacles for you for the moment, you can at least understand the scope of the trouble, create a little healthy space for yourself, and choose to move in the direction of what nourishes and sustains you in your faith.

Reconsidering the church in these chapters may also have reminded you of what you appreciate and value in your identity as a Christian and a Catholic. No matter how difficult our committed relationships become, working on them is always preferable as a first resort and ending them an option held out for when all else fails. If you come to the conclusion that there is much in the tradition of the church worth hanging on to, you may be ready to attempt reentry into the church at the parish level.

In order to reconsider the front door of the parish, however, it's good to keep the back door in sight. Until recently no one has been formally paying attention to the back door of the church through which such large numbers have exited—their stories untold, their wounds unaddressed. As with any relationship, we cannot kiss and make up until the real issues of hurt and injury have been named and acknowledged. As Archbishop Michael Sheehan of Santa Fe, New Mexico, has said, "I believe that we are so busy taking care of the people who come to church that many parishes have not taken the time and energy to think about the people who don't come" ("Take Note," *Catholic Trends,* 12 October 2002, 2). But in the last two decades a startling and hopeful phenomenon has emerged, what amounts to a movement of ministry for returning Catholics. Carrie Kemp in Minnesota has sustained a creative and healing ministry of welcoming the faithful back to the church in "Catholics Coming Home" programs, which have sprouted up in parishes across the country. The Paulist Fathers sponsor "Landings" meetings for wanderers looking for a place to return and be heard. On the national level the North American Forum on the Catechumenate, known for its process in bringing adult converts to baptism and full communion with the church, also promotes the rituals of "Re-Membering Church" in many dioceses for those seeking a formal process of reconciliation and reunion with the community of faith. If the back door of the church still has your attention, these programs are available in small-community settings for those who need to tell their story, address an injustice, get accurate information, and be finally heard and understood by representatives of the church.

For some, reentering the life of the parish cannot be considered without a public acknowledgment of the separation and the trouble that preceded it. Such programs as the three noted above can facilitate that process. But for others, being absent from the church may have been less of a crisis, and the possibility of return may be more a matter of will. Several books have been written to assist alienated or questioning Catholics in a reappraisal of their place in the church. These books may be useful for individuals or discussion groups. At the end of this book you will find a section of resources to help you connect to programs and publications available to those reconsidering Catholicism.

HOW TO READ A PARISH

Those who have moved around the country—in the service of a company or the military or just because they like change—will already be familiar with the business of learning the ropes in a new situation. In each new town, you have to find out the location of the closest supermarket, pharmacy, hospital, and, depending on your interests, the nearest school, entertainment, or good coffee shop. It might be critical for you to know which theater has good matinee prices. Another member of your family may be more concerned with finding the best Chinese takeout or the best comic-book rack. And if there's no good ice-cream stand within driving distance, some of us will just pack up and leave town altogether.

Different factors come into play when choosing a parish that's right for you, but the dynamics of separating out the crucial from the merely convenient still apply. In our discussion of the five models of church in chapter 4, you may have identified certain aspects of your engagement with religion that are nonnegotiable for you. It may be good preaching or uplifting music that compels you. You may be more interested in the friendliness of the community or the inclusion of children in the activities of the parish. You may be looking for the best possible worship experience on Sunday morning, or you may really want a community bubbling with activities and service opportunities seven days a week. Identifying your needs and being able to separate them from your preferences is very important. Depending on where you live, you may be able to find everything you want, or you may have to make some concessions. If scoring a perfect ten on your list of parish preferences is of primary value to you, you may have to move to an area that has more options available. Southern Utah does offer a lovely drive to the north rim of the Grand Canyon, but your choices for a Catholic parish in that part of the country may be limited.

Finding the right parish is like good detective work: it involves tracking down leads offered by various sources, researching, examining key information, and allowing for a certain amount of serendipity. It could be as simple as picking up a book like Paul Wilkes's *Excellent Catholic Parishes* (New York: Paulist Press, 2001) and discovering a dynamic church listed in your area. Or you may have a coworker who raves about the vitality of her Sunday experience. If you begin your reentry into the church through a parish program for returning Catholics, that may be a sign that such a parish is aware of your particular needs and is sensitive to them. In the absence of such leads, you may have to pick up the phone book and start attending the Catholic parishes listed one by one.

But what are you looking for? How can you read the clues that every parish provides about its self-understanding? Here are a few things you can consider in the search for the best fit for you. Relying on any one of these factors could be misleading, but together they suggest the nature of a community and its leadership. The first source of information doesn't even involve personal contact, if you are especially shy about diving back in. Just pick up a bulletin, available in the back of most churches. You can learn a lot about what's going on at a parish and who's in charge just by what's there and what's not.

The parish bulletin is a cornucopia of information. Many parishes now have a mission statement right on the cover of their bulletins that explains how they perceive their purpose. Here is one that tells you rather precisely what the intentions of the community are:

WE WELCOME . . . people of all faiths and all races, divorced or separated persons, families with children, gays and lesbians, homeless people, loving relationships, married couples, single persons, those in recovery, travelers from far and near, widows and widowers, visitors.

WE SEEK . . . to live the Gospel of Jesus Christ, to gather the Community and Tell the Story, to Break the Bread and Share the Cup.

WE TREASURE OUR PAST, WE HOPE IN THE FUTURE. (Holy Spirit Newman Hall Parish, Berkeley, California, from a 2002 bulletin)

That description may sound like God's kingdom come or your biggest nightmare, depending on what you're looking for, but no one can say the community hasn't been clear about who they are striving to be. Here's another that provides a different but equally honest statement of purpose:

WE ARE A COMMUNITY OF BELIEVERS founded on St. Peter and the Holy Apostles of Jesus Christ, who is Lord and

Savior. We are true to our Catholic Christian heritage, especially in honoring the Mother of God and the Saints of God. We are dedicated to building the kingdom of God in our world, committed to each other as a family of brothers and sisters, drawing our strength from the celebration of the Eucharist, embarked together on a great adventure of faith. (St. Christopher of the Desert Church, Joshua Tree, California, from a 2002 bulletin)

Some parish mission statements emphasize that a parish is interested in fostering a spirit of prayer and holiness in its membership (we can read the mystery model of church here). Others will list their outreach programs and service to the poor (servant model), or their allegiance to the teachings of the church (institution model), or the kind of people they are striving together to be (community model), or their dedication to the word of God and an evangelizing witness (herald model). The mission statement of a parish, even when it's advertised on the bulletin cover, isn't necessarily the last word on the subject of parish identity. (It could have been written by the previous administration.) But when it's offered, it pays to take a look at it.

Other, more subtle cues within the bulletin may support or counter the mission statement or serve in lieu of that statement for those that don't offer one. One bulletin may alert you to no less than three fundraisers going on this week in the parish—is this the primary focus of their efforts? Another may be bi- or trilingual, an indication of the varied composition of the assembly. A third may be monopolized by clergy announcements with headings like "Deacon's Corner," "Father Bill's Appointments," "Pastor's Last Word," and so on. Still another bulletin may be all about the news at the parochial school, which may be something that excites or depresses you, depending on your state in life.

What organizations are gathering for meetings: the Knights of Columbus, the Rosary Altar Society, a social justice study group, the liturgy committee, recovery or support groups? What kind of prayer opportunities may be offered besides Mass: the rosary, contemplative prayer, charismatic groups, Taizé-style ecumenical prayer around the cross? Are there adult education classes, evenings of reflection, Bible studies, guest speakers? Is the parish staff large or small? Does it encompass laypeople and clergy, or are the same three people listed as chairing every committee? Finally, and perhaps most significantly, is anybody ever *thanked* in the bulletin for what they did: contributing to the collection, showing up to decorate the church, turning out for the Mexican dinner?

A bulletin may seem like just a sheet of announcements, but the longer you spend looking at it, the more you will see it reveals the tone of the leadership and community behind it.

THE BUILDING SENDS A MESSAGE

Any individual bulletin may send an imperfect signal about what goes on in the parish, so it wouldn't be fair to disregard a community on the basis of just one copy. (Unless it's a particularly bad one—a two-page rant about Father Bob's latest gripe would be enough warning to stay away from that church, at least until there's a regime change.) But the church facility also tells us a lot about what a particular church is about. Obviously, older churches may have a Byzantine architectural style and modern churches an unfortunate tendency to look like geodesic domes. The outward appearances may be distressing to lovers of the traditional or contemporary style, but the look of a church is more about taste than content. What really communicates the tone of a parish is not the style of its building but some other factors that may at first escape us.

For example, what is the sum total of the church complex? Most Catholic parishes are not composed of just a church but may also include a rectory, convent, school, church hall, or cemetery. Especially in older parishes, those buildings once came with the territory; but as schools and convents closed or new needs arose, there may have been a reallocation of space for small-group meetings or parishwide gatherings. How much of the property is today at the service of the largest share of the population? If there is no place for the parish to gather or no small rooms available on church property for lay groups to use, that sends a message that such gatherings are not considered important or are not on the agenda.

New churches are often built with gathering spaces in mind, but even older churches can be renovated to facilitate the sense that the people really *are* the church. Some parishes have removed a few pews in the back of the church to open an area around the baptismal font for greater participation or simply for gathering before or after Mass. This demonstrates an awareness that the parish is a real community and not just a group of people riding the same train home. Room in various locations of the church for people with wheelchairs or other mobility problems is another architectural cue that such folks are not relegated to the back of the assembly (if they can get into the church at all) or forced to sit right in front in order to be "out of the way" of the communion lines. How many Catholics do you know who like to sit in front?

In the same way, a church with no stained-glass windows, few or no statues of saints, and a cross with no Christ on it sends a message that the church is not well suited to persons attracted to traditional devotions. On the other hand, a church with four images of the Blessed Virgin Mary within the sight lines of the altar gives the impression that those who are uncomfortable with traditional piety may want to look elsewhere.

Other concerns might involve the worship space: Can everybody see and hear from where they're sitting—and does anybody care if they can't? Is the worship space suitable to the needs of modern participatory liturgy, or is it a hindrance to serving the people adequately? Is there a place of prominence for each of these pieces of liturgical furniture: the altar, the pulpit, the tabernacle, and the baptismal font? If any of these is less visible or ornate than the presider's chair, there may be a problem.

TESTING OUT A NEW PARISH

Perusing the parish bulletin and snooping around the property will give you some information about a prospective parish, but it won't tell you everything. Those measures are just the initial "sniff" test that inevitably leads to actual Mass attendance, which is the litmus test for most of us. Many who have been away from church for a while feel uneasy about crashing the Sunday service unannounced, so to speak, after all this time. So they may prefer to attend a daily Mass, which is smaller, quieter, and seems less demanding all around.

It should be noted that the daily Mass crowd has quite a different character than the Sunday assembly. Such groups are often less formal with each other because they see one another in closer quarters and on a regular basis. If someone is missing for a day or two, another person may check up to make sure the missing parishioner is not sick or in need. In an urban setting many of these folks may work in the same offices or, if retired, live in the same neighborhood. The pace of the service will be quicker, with little or no music, fewer readings, and often no homily by the priest, in consideration of those who are on their way to work, or on lunch break, or on their way home, depending on the time of day. Those who view music or preaching as an indispensable part of their worship experience may find the daily Mass experience somewhat lacking. On the other hand, it's a terrific way to learn about the bare-bones practice of the liturgy itself, when attention to the prayers and the dialogue of our responses can be much more focused. The smaller assembly may feel friendlier, and we may sense in the reception of the sacrament the intimacy of our communion as well as the deliberate act of our witness.

Finding a parish that understands how to create good liturgy—and conversely, coming to an appreciation of liturgy within ourselves—is one reliable way to find our place within the church. Like most things, ritual in general and the Mass in particular can be approached legalistically (by measuring the distance between the candlesticks to ensure it's orthodox, for example). But that's not what we mean here by good liturgy. Sometimes the best liturgies bend the rules in order to create a greater sense of community for the local assembly. What counts for good taste in liturgy also varies considerably. It's the difference between the style of your living room versus that of your grandmother's parlor. It may be best to suspend personal preferences here in favor of creating an environment where everyone has a sense of sacred space and communion with God and others.

Sometimes that means letting go of a pet peeve for the sake of greater unity. For example, in some churches the pastor may adopt a little ritual that seems idiosyncratic and distracting—like the priest who leads the assembly in reciting the Hail Mary right after reading the Gospel. It doesn't technically "belong" in the Mass, but this thing that annoys the heck out of you may be what makes others feel personally engaged with the leader of the assembly and the ritual itself. One may consider this an opportunity to shoot off a letter to the bishop about liturgical abuses—or to practice Christian charity and allow this idiosyncrasy its place. What is most important in the worship of the church is not ritual perfection, or even flawless and charismatic leadership, but those things that contribute to the spirit of our gathering: hospitality and a sense of welcome; thoughtfulness and care on the part of all who minister at the altar; mindfulness of what we are doing as an assembly; and active participation that engages us as believers in the profession of our faith.

Every piece of the liturgy has its part to play in drawing us to the heart of our unity in Christ. A parish where the Scripture readings are *proclaimed,* not dully read or overdramatically performed, reminds us that this is God's word announced to us. When preaching focuses on the Scripture readings and reveals the human and divine realities of God's word, we know this is not a mere lesson in morality but a declaration of the good news of Jesus Christ among us. Where musicians have the necessary skills and enable us to "pray twice" in our singing, as St. Augustine urged us to do, we enjoy the richness of joining our voices together in praise. In parishes where the leaders and planners of worship let the rituals do what they were intended to do and where the people participate with attention, enthusiasm, and devotion, we feel the power implicit in rituals that have accompanied religious expression from ancient times. When what we do together in our worship points not to itself but to the great and mysterious interchange between God and human beings, we have found a home in the Mass. All the conditions mentioned above, and others, keep us coming back to the kind of worship that transforms us, connects us to the church and its mission, and surrounds us with the abundant and unique gifts that Catholic liturgy has to offer.

Paying attention to the liturgy itself—how it's led and how folks participate in return—may bring us to a different or deeper understanding of the church as a whole. We may begin to ask new questions of ourselves about what we want from the church and what we are looking for in a worshiping community.

PREACHING IS KEY

The quality of preaching comes up again and again as a key issue for both practicing Catholics and those who have left, or are thinking of leaving, the church. (For the record, this is a big complaint in many Protestant congregations too.) How good or bad the preaching is on Sundays makes a big difference in the value folks put on going to Mass. Some preachers are intent on extracting ethical demands from the readings and imposing them on the congregation, rather than communicating what God's fresh and living word has to say to us. The modern Catholic homily differs from the classic style of a sermon in that it is not meant to be a moral lesson or a time for teaching catechism but rather a weekly opportunity to announce the good news of Jesus Christ. Regretfully, some of what we hear isn't very good news.

Besides moralistic content, some homilies also suffer from poor delivery. Quite simply, some who serve as priests and deacons just don't have the charism, or innate gift, for preaching. And as odd as it may seem, until recently many seminaries did not offer much training in public speaking or preaching beyond a fundamental course or two. Preachers were therefore on their own to a great extent, learning by doing and mostly by imitating the preaching style of priests they had known. This is why some preachers may seem distant and impersonal and others too chatty and casual. They may not have been taught to pay enough attention to their tone of voice or posture, and they may never vary them. They may not know how to establish a genuine conversation with the congregation or to communicate a sense of humor and compassion. For all these reasons it may be difficult to see the person of faith behind the homilist.

When you find a parish where the preacher's "got gift" and the homilies are uplifting, engaging, and transforming, rejoice and stay put! But even the most halting and hesitant preacher may have something to offer, so a quick rush to judgment isn't always the best policy. A woman tells of the time she was visiting a church in Texas where the priest, a small and soft-spoken man, seemed quite frightened of his role, standing in his robes like someone in front of a firing squad. She was tempted to tune him out at homily time, but then she heard that gentle little voice at the microphone say, "God loves you." It was a simple phrase, hardly original, and yet he said it with such tenderness that it sounded absolutely profound. The assembly, who knew their priest better than she did, leaned forward with an outpouring of loving assent that was almost tangible. The visitor was moved to tears by the end of an uncreative but entirely pure expression of how our hearts seek and are sought by the heart of God.

Even when you think the preacher has little to offer and hardly seems able to rise to the task at hand, you can use the time to create your own "homily moment." You can find in the Scripture readings key words that jump out at you and express your faith, the realities of your life, or an inspiring new way to see your relationship with God. This is God speaking to you in the divine word and certainly is not an illegitimate way of "listening" to the homily. You may reflect on your own life and the situation of your family, community, and world. You may want to take up the habit of reading the Sunday Scripture yourself during the week, maybe with the help of a Bible commentary. (See the resources section for a list of aids to reading Scripture.) You can effectively compose your own homily in your head while sitting through a less appealing one—many worshipers over the years have used this crucial survival skill. And it's also a good opportunity to exercise the virtue of compassion for those who have been called to minister but are not necessarily gifted to preach. It's helpful to give the preacher the benefit of the doubt: he may be *wonderfully* suited to other aspects of his calling, like St. John Vianney, who was a failure as a seminary student, and an unremarkable preacher and administrator, but the best confessor who ever lived.

BEING OPEN TO SURPRISE

When we define the notion of the "good parish" in a narrow way— as one with a terrific music program or a well-developed social outreach—we may miss the other gifts a community has that may summon us to spiritual growth or call forth our own response of leadership and service. If stations-of-the-cross spirituality has never been part of your experience, you may be surprised to find that devotional practices can be very effective aids to recollection and prayer. If the idea of a guitar Mass makes you faint in horror, you may discover that the words to some of those songs are moving and memorable. If your first choice would be to stay as far away from a social justice group as possible, joining a parish with a strong commitment to community outreach may offer you the opportunity to receive a new heart for the poor Christ. If Mass for you so far has been mainly about the preaching, an uninspiring homilist may prompt you to look more deeply into the meaning of communion in your relationship with the Sunday assembly: how that young man with the long braid, the couple with the three rambunctious kids, and the old woman in the flowered dress are part of the Body of Christ along with you.

Living in a free society, we are not often challenged to move beyond our tastes and comfort zone. But Christian spirituality requires us to continually stretch "outside the box" to grow beyond personal security and ease for the radical work of the gospel, which makes the last first, the least greatest, and the poor rejoice. The "good parish," then, may not be the one we would choose for ourselves for the most enjoyable hour each Sunday but the one that will offer us room to consider a new aspect of the Body of Christ. Each new community of the faithful calls us to bring forward our selves, our witness, and our gifts for the sake of the whole church. Though we may not be accustomed to thinking about church in terms other than what we *want,* the idea that we may be called to a parish because of what we *bring* is worth considering.

Approaching the search for a home parish from the perspective of "call" rather than "designer fit" may be the best way to find the place that's good for us to be. The Newman Centers, which minister to college communities, will often be lively and experimental, and the cathedral parishes will generally be regal and dignified; but in between lies the rest of the church, in a remarkable mix of seeking and finding the way of Jesus, which is "the way, the truth, and the life" for believers. If that's the community you're looking for, seek and you will find!

In our next chapter we will be looking into the matter of spiritual hunger and how to feed it. For those who left the church because of an inability to meet this need, as well as for those who are still in the pews but are gnawing on the bones of an insufficient spiritual life, we offer a few directions you might take to find what has been lacking.

SEVEN

Strengthening Your Spiritual Life

Most people who go to church, and just about everybody who doesn't, can agree on at least one thing: mere church attendance isn't enough to sustain a vital life of faith. Outward rituals of commitment, whether in religion or any other significant relationship, are not complete unless they express what's going on deep down in a person's life. In fact, the outward sign of ritual only makes sense if it comes as a result of a whole and entire commitment to which the sign bears witness in the public act of worship.

Some will ask the chicken-and-egg question: which comes first, the pledge of faith or the experience of it? The usual answer applies: either and both. In church practice we baptize babies who don't even have language skills to express their experience of anything, much less the faith of the church. In this case, it is the faith of the parents and their intentions of passing on their belief that stand in for the child's personal pledge. At the same time, the church also has a process known as the Rite of Christian Initiation of Adults, or RCIA, which assists people who have already had a faith awakening and are seeking to give it expression within the life of the church. So, as we can see in relationship to church membership itself, some begin with the pledge and others the experience.

The deeper truth behind the which-comes-first issue is "both-and." The pledge of faith cannot give us faith, nor can the experience of the sacred alone make us faithful. But the two together supply what is lacking so that both can reach their fullest meaning. Whichever end of the equation we find ourselves on—religious commitment or religious experience—it is necessary to stretch for the other. As the saints declared in word and deed, "Live faith until you have faith." Just as in a marriage pledge, we recognize that there is love before the commitment but a deeper love as a result of the commitment. So too our pledge to be faithful people supports us in becoming ever more faithful.

Perhaps one of the basic sources of religious alienation is being top-heavy on the commitment side of our relationship to the church while the experience side remains relatively weightless. Where can we go to acquire some ballast for the spiritual life?

WHAT IS SPIRITUALITY?

The spiritual quest is, at its heart, the search for meaning. Humans have traveled down many paths to acquire this meaning and to get answers for life's big questions. For those who choose a specifically religious path, however, the spiritual quest becomes very focused. The simplest way to speak of the religious quest is that it begins and ends with the total centering of our lives around God. Or perhaps we should say that we discover that we live and move and have our being, now and forever, within the life of God. Our essential understanding of this reality, our spirituality, obviously cannot be merely one element of our lifestyle; it *is* our lifestyle. Spirituality describes the lifelong process to respond to the presence of God in all things: in the work we do, within our significant relationships, through the inner movements of our hearts, amid our desires and actions and decisions, in all the things we make important in our lives by devoting our time and energy to them.

As Evelyn, a lifelong Catholic, sums it up: "There's no place where I stop being Christian and start being something else. It's how I think and the way I make decisions. It's how I love and why I choose to love the people I do. I'm not just here in this world making money and doing time. I am here to *live* my life and to fulfill the call God put in me."

A healthy and vital spirituality defines who we are and helps us to grow and develop along the way of faith. The way we express our spirituality should be a support and a consolation to us; it should also afford enough challenge to keep us moving forward and to help us avoid complacence. Naturally, not everyone needs the same things in order to mature in faith, nor do we all receive comfort from the same resources, because of our different personalities and life stories. In this sense, the Catholic Church has something for every spiritual journey and personal need. The spiritual practices of Catholicism cross many centuries, cultures, and expressions of faith. They incorporate paths first explored by people as diverse as Anthony of the Desert, who fought with his demons alone in the wild; Bernard of Clairvaux, who formed his monks in a life of prayer and community; Catherine of Siena, who had marvelous supernatural revelations but also had the pragmatic gumption to argue publicly with popes; Elizabeth of Hungary, a wife and mother who still found time to care for her neighbor; Frédéric Ozanam, a layman who started the Society of St. Vincent de Paul on behalf of the poor; and Dorothy Day, who was committed to both political and spiritual answers to social ills.

The Catholic spiritual tradition is a rich heritage that leads down countless paths toward our common meeting ground in the life of God. The church can provide real nourishment for spiritual hunger, and Catholic spirituality may open a door of reentry for those who have felt disconnected or shut out. If you are uncertain about how or where to begin, here are some common starting points to consider in forming your own spiritual path within the life of the church.

SACRAMENTS: OUR WINDOWS ON THE WORLD

We have already talked about how the sacraments are the touchstones of being Catholic and belonging to the church. But sacraments are a lot more. They teach us how to see the world and trace God's presence within our experience.

Christian tradition affirms the sacredness of the world, which has its origin in God, who created it. Catholicism holds to the belief that all of creation is a living sign of God and can teach us about the One who is the source of life itself. Because the world comes from the hand of God, creation as a whole is a vessel for the sacred.

A question might be raised: if the whole world is good, holy, and beautiful, then why do we celebrate the sacraments of the church? Not to replace the holiness of the world, or to upstage it, certainly. The sacraments act as a sevenfold prism for the divine light that shines in every aspect of creation. The word *sacrament* means something dedicated to or representative of the sacred. Through the ritual of the sacraments, those taking part in the celebration encounter the presence of God in an action that encompasses our personal testimony of faith as well as our public service to one another. (The word *liturgy* means an act of public service, for our communal celebration of faith supports the whole church and gives witness to those outside of it.)

Each sacrament is a unique affirmation of the sacredness of the world and human life and a testimony to our communion with the God who made and sustains it all. Sacraments are also formal occasions when all the principal parties of the religious encounter are assembled: God, the people of God along with their ministers, and the natural elements of the world shaped and touched by the work of human hands—bread, wine, water, oil, garments, and precious metals. The sacraments highlight peak moments of the human experience: birth, growing up and participating in community, marriage, communion with God, dedicating oneself to service, the need for forgiveness, and the hope of rescue in times of sickness and the hour of death. Sacraments raise the most basic human experiences to the life of God and show how God's life is already present in them.

Consider, for example, what the sacrament of baptism teaches us about initiation, welcome, and belonging. Baptism gives us our birth into the church through the outpouring of water, the source of life. Water nourishes, soothes, cleans, and refreshes. Those of us who pass through this water become part of one another in the church and also sharers in the body of Christ. We are cleansed, made whole, and renewed for a fresh start.

But water is likewise a potentially destructive force, which St. Paul makes clear: "Or are you unaware that we who were baptized into Christ Jesus were baptized into his death? We were indeed buried with him through baptism into death, so that, just as Christ was raised from the dead by the glory of the Father, we too might live in newness of life" (Rom 6:3–4 NAB). Stories illustrating both these aspects of the power of water abound in Scripture:

it saved the Israelites in the desert, who were dying of thirst, but it drowned those overcome by the flood in Noah's time. The dual forces at work in the symbol of water remind us that life is a process of birthing and dying, and we must die to ourselves, many times over, in order to live the greater life to which we are invited. In this way, baptism gives us a window onto the reality of paradox: how death gives way to life, how the least can become greatest, and how humility is the path to glory.

Each sacrament in turn offers its grace in the moment of reception and becomes a metaphor for understanding our way in the world in larger terms. The Eucharist is a meal of bread and wine that makes us one with the divine life of Jesus Christ. We incorporate the body and blood of Christ and are likewise incorporated into his Body. And we who participate in this meal become one with each other as well as with Christ, sharing one life in this tangible sign. The image of the meal instructs us to look to the hunger of the world—physical and spiritual—and directs us to respond to these needs in works of charity, justice, and evangelization. Because of the centrality of this meal to the life of the Christian, we recognize that all human hunger is an opportunity to come to know God and to serve the poor Christ in one another. Because the symbol of the meal is also basic to our lives, we are reminded that God has chosen to be revealed in simple moments, and therefore common things hold sacred realities for us to discover.

In the sacrament of confirmation, we accept the call to follow Christ in our maturity and to be anointed (literally "Christed," since *Christ* means "anointed one"). Often in this ritual we take on a new name and acknowledge a new identity as a disciple and servant. We learn how names call forth different aspects of our personality, and we reflect on how our surname calls us to belong to one family and our Christian name to a much larger identity. We embrace the gifts of the Holy Spirit (wisdom, understanding, knowledge, counsel, fortitude, reverence, and wonder in God's presence, adapted from Is 11:2–3) and strive to nurture the fruits of the Spirit (love, joy, peace, patience, kindness, generosity, faithfulness, gentleness, and self-control, as St. Paul tells us in Gal 5:22–23). Our vocation to follow Christ is demonstrated in acts of service that utilize the gifts and reveal the fruits of the Spirit implanted within us.

Reconciliation reminds us that we are sinners and we are forgiven, two inseparable realities of the Christian worldview. As recipients of God's compassion, we are summoned to be instruments of the divine compassion in our dealings with others. As we have seen with the other sacramental moments, the ritual sacrament reveals the ongoing process to which we are called and the deeper truth underlying the world around us. Forgiveness isn't something we find and leave in the confessional booth; it's an orientation we take with us as grateful people. If we know ourselves to be forgiven, we will live with open hearts toward all the other imperfect people we meet, including ourselves.

Marriage and holy orders are particular expressions of the more general vocation we have already answered in confirmation. As followers of Christ, we spend our lives in service, and within the call to marriage or holy orders, we dedicate that service within the framework of particular relationships. Each partnership results in the mutual nurturing of life in families or communities, and all for the sake of bringing the love of Christ more effectively into the world. These relationships in turn reveal to us how *all* of our relationships, whether sacramentally inaugurated or not, are infused with the life of Christ and are opportunities for loving service. The sacramental sign always points to the greater reality present all around us, so that we might not miss it.

The final sacrament of anointing of the sick is a significant recollection that, in the end, it is not what we *do* but who we *are* as the children of God that is the point of our existence. In times of sickness, disability, and death, we touch our mortal limits and learn that being productive is neither the only purpose of our lives nor the most important one. Often we are tempted to place the emphasis of our days on what we get done, and yet the summons to be still and know who God is remains. We also learn in the season of suffering that God chose to be revealed in the person of the suffering Christ and that we follow Jesus as closely in the occasion of physical weakness and pain as we do in our most generous acts of service. In fact, here too, in the hour of human frailty, we serve God as well as in any other hour! It is a powerful statement we make when we accept the anointing of the sick and allow our weakness to testify to the sufficiency of God.

Often we limit and marginalize the experience of the sacraments by thinking of them as something that happens only in church, easily disconnected from the rest of life. It would be inappropriate to regard a sacrament as a spiritual "thing" to be handed out by the clergy and "received" by the rest of us. But the sacraments really teach us how to live. Vatican II called the Eucharist the "source and summit" of Christian life: *source,* because from it Christian life flows out; *summit* because it is what life heads toward. Participating in the sacraments is an opportunity for transformation of ourselves and our point of view.

Because the sacramental way of seeing is so important, our celebration of the sacraments should be a life-giving experience. This makes it essential for Catholics to locate a parish, Catholic campus ministry center, cathedral church, or other worshiping community where the sacraments are celebrated in ways that let their rich meaning shine forth.

GET A PRAYER LIFE

The public rituals of the church are guideposts for all of life, but what we do publicly must also be reinforced and affirmed by our personal practices. Although Catholic liturgy is by nature a formal exchange of ritual words and signs, how we exercise our spiritual life privately is entirely up to us. But whatever form we choose, prayer of some kind is considered a basic first step.

Prayer is simply turning to God. Anything that helps us orient ourselves to God can be a form of prayer. Thus the variety of prayer forms: spoken, silent, composed, spontaneous, long, short, even *being prayerful*—the attitude of responding to God's presence in everything we do.

Catholicism has recognized how prayer is both personal (something each of us does) and social (something we do with others). Whether praying alone, with another person or a small group, or with a lot of people as in the context of Mass, when Catholics pray, it is something both intensely private and something that is done in union (we say "in communion") with the whole church.

It's important to find a style of prayer that is appealing and suitable to your circumstances. (Historically, there was a group of folks who stood on pillars for long periods of time in prayer, but that may be an unlikely spiritual practice for a mother of three children.) Some of the most common Catholic prayer practices are praying with Scripture; praying the Liturgy of the Hours, the rosary, or the stations of the cross; using contemplative prayer; and invoking the intercession of the saints. Any of these practices is suitable for prayer, whether solitary, with a partner, or in a group.

Praying with Scripture

Scripture-based prayer has the advantage of letting the word of God speak first. Some brave souls may begin with Genesis and read a chapter a week, but that is not a method for the faint of heart. There are many page-a-day Scripture books available in Catholic bookstores, especially during the seasons of Lent and Advent, with passages of the Bible conveniently preselected for thoughtful meditation. But as Catholicism follows a predetermined set of readings for Sundays and weekdays, it is just as easy to acquire a Catholic calendar from your parish or an ordo (a booklet of the prescribed readings) from a Catholic bookstore and follow along with the whole church. Many parish Sunday bulletins also list the readings for the following week (sneak into the church vestibule and pick up a bulletin from last Sunday), and some Bibles and several Web sites give the daily readings as well (see the U.S. Catholic bishops' Web site at www.usccb.org).

One simple way of praying with the Bible is the ancient practice of *lectio divina,* or "holy reading." Once you have a passage from the Bible you want to pray with, start by asking for God's help in making the message of Scripture part of your life. Come up with your own prayer, or use the traditional prayer to the Holy Spirit: "Come, Holy Spirit, fill the hearts of your faithful and enkindle in them the fire of your love." Next read the Scripture passage. Then read it again as slowly as you can, noticing what speaks to you most personally. Turn over in your mind what has struck you, the story or an image or maybe even one word, and talk with God about its significance for your life. Praying with Scripture helps you see the

Bible as a book alive with the presence of God's spirit and not as a faraway history of exotic people and events.

The Liturgy of the Hours

Another prayer form, based on the Psalms, is called the Liturgy of the Hours, which also comes from the ancient church. The prayers for each day are contained in a book or series of books known as the breviary, and you can purchase the entire breviary or a variety of shorter and simpler forms of it in one volume. Originally a prayer practice of monks and clergy, the Liturgy of the Hours became available to the whole church after Vatican II. The Liturgy of the Hours provides up to five opportunities to pray daily, the principal times being morning and evening, along with midmorning, midday, midafternoon, and night. Each "hour" consists mostly of psalms, responses, short prayers, intercessions, a brief Scripture reading, and the Lord's Prayer. But you don't have to pray all of them every day. Praying even one of the hours reminds you of God's presence throughout the day as well as the sacred character of each hour that is given to us. Jesus told his disciples "about their need to pray always and not to lose heart" (Lk 18:1 NRSV), and St. Paul said simply, "Pray without ceasing" (1 Thes 5:17 NRSV). In the midst of the busyness that consumes the day, the Liturgy of the Hours creates some space for us to "pray always." For those who are just beginning to pray the Liturgy of the Hours, the best advice is to find a group that regularly prays it in your parish. Some parishes pray it before daily Mass together. Others may have a small group that joins together in the rectory, convent, or local retreat center that is open to the public.

The Rosary

The rosary is a beloved prayer that owes much to the monastic tradition of the Liturgy of the Hours and an equal part to the practice of meditation. The rosary began in response to the felt need of those townspeople who wanted to participate in the great spiritual work of prayer as practiced by the local monasteries but who could not for several practical reasons. Obviously, the time commitment a monk makes to prayer is different than what a person committed to the life of the family can offer. But there were also practical considerations: the scarcity of books and the fact that most people could not read. As the monks prayed their way through the 150 psalms of the Bible, the average person took to praying a simple prayer, recited 150 times over as he or she went about the work of the day, to join with the prayer rising from the church as a whole.

The rosary emerged from that practice in many different forms that eventually became formalized around fifteen mysteries regarding the person of Jesus as recalled through the experience of his mother, Mary. Today, since the promulgation of five additional mysteries of light by Pope John Paul II, which encompass the public ministry of Jesus, we now have twenty meditations on which to build our common prayer. The beauty of the rosary has always been its accessibility and malleability to fit any circumstance. The mysteries of the rosary can usually be purchased on a simple prayer card that you can slip into your pocket and consult after each "decade," or recitation of ten Hail Marys. You can choose to pray one set of five mysteries, which takes about fifteen minutes, or the entire set of twenty mysteries, which can take an hour. You can pray the rosary quietly on public transit by fingering the beads in your pocket to keep count, or you can set aside some special time during the day to sit in a favorite spot for fruitful meditation. The mantra of the rosary is remarkably suitable for entering deep prayer states and becomes a natural choice as a prayer of petition for the needs of others and the world, a prayer based on groups of concerns that are joyful, sorrowful, and glorious, or a prayer for those in need of the revealing light of Christ.

The Stations of the Cross

A prayer form that is most often associated with the season of Lent, the Way of the Cross (as it is formally called) is a prayer for all seasons. The idea of this prayer came from the ancient practice of pilgrimage. Some who had particular spiritual burdens to discharge, penances to do, or needs to intercede for would make the long journey to the Holy Land on foot in search of the special graces attached to the land where Christ had walked. Obviously, this took considerable time and resources to accomplish, and not everyone could make the journey even once in a lifetime. But the spiritual benefits of a pilgrimage were enormous, not the least of which was the community that often spontaneously formed along the way for protection, mutual encouragement, and fellowship. The final leg of the journey was to follow the Via Dolorosa, or Way of Sadness—the route that Jesus presumably took through Jerusalem to Calvary with his cross. It was this final stage of pilgrimage that led to the idea of the stations, or stops, that Jesus took along that last sad street.

The stations of the cross became standardized over time, encompassing at last the fourteen stops we have today (fifteen if the Resurrection is included). Originally, the franchise of the stations belonged to the Franciscan order, who were the guardians of the Holy Land. At Franciscan parishes and retreat centers, anyone unable to make an actual pilgrimage to the Holy Land was invited to symbolically journey through those fateful stops and make the same reparations and intercessions that other pilgrims made. Today almost every Catholic parish has a specially installed group of stations, and many retreat centers will have outdoor stations as well. By walking the stations one can literally "move" toward spiritual wholeness. We can understand our spiritual lives as a journey toward greater integrity through accompanying the passion of Jesus by this wholly engaging prayer. We can use one of the many books of meditations on the stations that have been written by spiritual masters to accompany us along the way, or we can simply offer our own prayers as we go.

Intercession of the Saints

Devotion to the saints may be an area where Catholics are most frequently and completely misunderstood. First of all, it should be said that we do not worship the saints: worship and adoration belong to God alone. Even Mary receives a particular honor in the church technically known as *hyperdulia,* which is a notch below adoration, even though it is a notch above the veneration we show to the average saint. It is also important to recognize that we do not pray *to* the saints; we ask for them to pray with us and to intercede for us before God. This makes sense in the context of whom we believe the saints to be: human beings who were especially close to God in life and who have demonstrated their capability of great love for and service to others. Their lives brought them so close to God that we believe their influence continues even after their death. Saints inspire us to imitate them, and lest we put them on too high a pedestal, we should recall the words of Dorothy Day, herself a candidate for official sainthood, who wrote, echoing St. Paul, "We are called to be saints" (*Catholic Worker,* April 1958).

Catholics believe that saints are also "patrons" of areas of life given over to their special care, usually because some aspect of their lives or deaths has something to do with a particular human activity, occupation, place, or need. For example, St. Francis of Assisi, who had a remarkable relationship to the natural world, is the patron saint of animals and ecology. St. Peregrine suffered from cancer and so is the patron saint of cancer sufferers. Our Lady of Guadalupe, who appeared to the Native American Juan Diego, is the patron of the Americas. If you are looking for a saint who has a special concern for your particular circumstances, lists of the patron saints appear in many Catholic reference books, like *The HarperCollins Encyclopedia of Catholicism* (see the resources section). And if you can't find a saint to hear you out, there's always St. Jude, the patron of lost causes.

A living relationship with a saint, nourished through prayer, gives us a companion whose earthly life inspires us and whose heavenly life gives us a friend in the communion of saints, which encompasses all living and deceased members of the church. Saints look out for us, help us, listen to our needs, and bring our prayers before God with intimate knowledge of the needs of earth and the possibilities of heaven.

Contemplative Prayer

So far, most of the prayer forms we've looked at rely on words and images to establish our communication with God. Contemplative prayer puts us in touch with the God of silence. Before God created the universe, there was utter silence, and that silence remains as God's "first language," like a backdrop to creation. In contemplative prayer we take some time to get behind the noise and busyness of the world and listen to the silence. There, too, we may hear the voice of God. "For God alone my soul waits in silence," says Psalm 62:1 (NRSV).

According to one method of contemplative prayer, you begin by asking the Holy Spirit to give you a "sacred word" that expresses your intention to accept God's presence and action. An example of a sacred word is *peace*. Sit comfortably with eyes closed, settle briefly, and then introduce the sacred word into your mind. When thoughts or images or sounds threaten to distract you, say the sacred word gently to yourself and thereby let go of the thoughts, returning to silence. Many people find twenty minutes a comfortable period of time for the experience of contemplation.

PRAYING IN COMMON

As we indicated, all of the forms of prayer above can be practiced alone or in groups. Some people will find themselves naturally drawn to private prayer, and others will seek a prayer partner or communal experience. Just as in the pursuit of physical exercise, the group experience is valuable for the added dimension of support, a disciplined time to gather, or the sense of being responsible to a community with your presence and participation.

The social dimension of prayer has a long history. From the earliest days of the church, Christians have come together to pray. In the book of Acts we read that the first Christians "were constantly devoting themselves to prayer" and that "the whole group of those who believed were of one heart and soul" (1:14, 4:32 NRSV).

The most obvious way to pray with others is in the daily or Sunday Eucharist. If you're going to church at this time, try this: during the week pray with Scripture noted for the upcoming Sunday. This practice will deepen your hearing of Scripture and your appreciation of the homily. Pray before Mass, asking God to open your heart, and afterward express gratitude for all God's gifts, especially the gift of Christ present in the Eucharist. Missalettes and hymnals in the pews contain prayers for before and after Mass; you may of course prefer to come up with prayers of your own. Most of all, put yourself in the frame of mind that everything you do in church on Sunday is prayer. Your singing, spoken prayers, silence, even your posture and how you greet other people—everything—can be prayer.

If you are looking for a smaller and more intimate experience of communal prayer, consider joining a prayer group or small faith community. Attending a small prayer group can be a good way to connect to a parish if you've been out awhile or feel marginalized in your present mode of attendance. Many parishes offer a faith-sharing program called RENEW, which gathers once or twice a month in people's homes. Call the parish secretary, who will either sign you up or direct you to the parish coordinator for RENEW. If your parish doesn't have such a program, there may be similar groups by other names—again, the parish secretary might be your best resource.

If the local parish can't help, some cities may have houses of prayer run by religious communities like the Franciscans, Benedictines, or Sisters of Mercy. If so, you should be able to find these prayer houses in the phone book; give them a call and see what kinds of prayer opportunities they offer. If there is a college community nearby, look to see if it has a Catholic Newman Center, which is often a storehouse of prayer experiences and lectures on spirituality. You can call the diocesan chancery or check on the Internet to find a list of prayer gatherings in your area.

If you are motivated to do so, you may even want to start your own prayer group. Gather a group of family and friends willing to meet on a regular basis. Rotate responsibility among the members of the group for leading the prayers for each session, which could include a short formal service, spontaneous prayer, meditation with Scripture, intercessory prayer for personal needs or the needs of the world, or even silent or contemplative prayer, as the preferences of the group dictate.

For some people the desire to meet with a regular group for a long-term commitment to spiritual growth could lead to interest in formally affiliating with a religious group as a tertiary. Those who belong to religious groups as tertiaries (also known as third orders) are *not* called to priesthood or religious life as celibates who take vows of poverty, chastity, and obedience. The third orders are composed of people who are attracted to the features of a religious group's spirituality (referred to as the group's charism, or spiritual gift) but choose to live it out in the midst of their families and secular obligations. Such people become attached as tertiary members to a group like the Carmelites, for example, and participate in the Carmelite lifestyle and receive guidance from members of the order while remaining fully "in the world." If a particular religious community attracts you (but not in such a way that you feel compelled to leave the circumstances of your present life behind), you may want to ask if they have a third order affiliated with their group.

SPIRITUAL DIRECTION: YOUR PERSONAL COMPASS

Like the Liturgy of the Hours, spiritual direction used to be largely the territory of priests and members of religious orders, but it is now practiced much more widely in the church, especially among laypeople. It is not a form of prayer, but it can be a useful practice for those who are seeking greater guidance in the business of prayer and spiritual growth.

In spiritual direction you meet regularly, perhaps once a month, with a person called a spiritual director, with whom you talk about how your prayer life is going, where you've been finding—or not finding—God in your life, and how you've been living out your faith. In the Catholic Church spiritual direction has the same confidentiality expectation as confession: a spiritual director must respect the confidentiality of what is said in direction.

God is already present and active in each person's life, but not all of us are used to tracing the patterns of divine activity. A spiritual director serves as a companion and guide to help you notice and express God's workings in your life. He or she may also support and challenge you in equal parts when you need sanctuary, on the one hand, or prodding on the other.

How do you find a spiritual director, and what should you look for in one? If you know a priest, religious sister or brother, or other church leader who has impressed you with his or her personal holiness, that's a great place to begin. These individuals may be willing either to direct you personally or refer you to someone who directs them. If you haven't met such a person, you may be able to get a referral from a local parish staff member, a friend who has been in spiritual direction, or some other knowledgeable person you trust. Without the personal first impression, you may have to do a little sorting and sifting in this method to find the right person. If you live within the vicinity of a retreat center, you may find many directors regularly available there. You may also try contacting Spiritual Directors International, an organization that does not recommend specific spiritual directors but will put you in touch with a regional representative, who can offer a list of possible directors in your area. (Spiritual Directors International is online at www.sdiworld.org.)

The next step will be to develop a list of potential directors and evaluate them. Meet with each of them once and try to find out if they have received training in spiritual direction; whether they are connected to a particular Christian tradition and, if so, which one; if they are in direction themselves; to whom, if anyone, they are accountable for the spiritual direction work they do (spiritual directors are *not* professionally certified, though quite a few professional training programs exist); and whether they charge fees (some do, if that's how they make their living; others don't, if they are not full-time directors, or else they may operate on a sliding scale). Look for someone who listens well, impresses you as a person of faith, and seems experienced in the spiritual life. Above all, find someone you can trust; after all, you will be sharing many aspects of your life with this person.

TAKE A RETREAT!

Even Jesus took a retreat once in a while. On several occasions Jesus felt the need to get away from it all and seek spiritual refreshment. We read that he "got up and went out to a deserted place, and there he prayed" (Mk 1:35 NRSV). On another occasion he "went up on the mountain to pray" (Mk 6:46 NRSV). Luke tells in his Gospel of how Jesus "would withdraw to deserted places and pray" (5:16 NRSV).

To "make" a retreat in the informal sense, some will simply go backpacking or to the beach. But if you want a little guidance and more focus for your experience, you can also go to a retreat house, which is specifically designed to provide this service. You can make a reservation by yourself or with others (as in a parish group, with friends, or your spouse), and you can stay for a day of recollection, a weekend, or longer. (To do the Spiritual Exercises of St. Ignatius of Loyola, for example, look for a Jesuit-run retreat center and expect to spend an extended period of time.) Retreat centers offer spiritual programs of great variety—highly structured or absolutely free and open, as you prefer. To consider a range of retreat options around the country, browse through a book like *Catholic America: Self-Renewal Centers and Retreats,* by Patricia Christian-Meyer (Santa Fe, N.Mex.: John Muir Publications, 1989). This guide gives you practical advice on the value of making a retreat, information on what kinds of experiences you can choose from, and a listing of centers in many states with descriptions of their programs and contact information.

Many retreat centers are run by Catholic religious orders, so you may find yourself at a monastery or convent out in the country or on a wooded estate. Facilities vary widely, but on average, you can expect to stay in a simple guest room, pay a modest daily fee, eat institutional food, and maybe share a bathroom. (You're not there for the accommodations, though some retreat centers are quite comfortable.) The real benefits of retreats lay in the time given over to prayer, rest, reading, worship, and sometimes talks given on spiritual subjects by retreat leaders or staff members of the retreat house. Priests, religious sisters or brothers, or laypeople may be available to offer you spiritual counseling on a one-on-one basis.

In a faith environment, away from the responsibilities and pressures of daily life, a retreat offers the opportunity to focus on what is most important in your spiritual life at this time: your relationship to God, others, your work, your life circumstances, or the church. It can help to go into the experience of retreat with a focused question, like "What would it mean for me to resume a relationship with the church at this time?" or "What changes do I have to make to my life at this crossroads in order to be more faithful?" Such a question can be addressed during a retreat in different ways: by asking God in prayer to supply an answer; by reading Scripture or other spiritual books that engage you in conversation; by grappling with your issue in daily talks with a retreat director; or simply by having some peace and quiet for sustained reflection.

And you don't even have to "go away" to make a retreat. In fact, you don't have to leave your computer. If you have access to the Internet, several excellent online retreats are available to walk you through spiritual reflection steps that don't demand a lot of time. (See the resources section for some suggestions.) With online retreats, you can participate in them from home or work, privately, at any time of the day or night, at whatever level of involvement you prefer.

IF AT FIRST YOU DON'T SUCCEED,
TRY SOMETHING ELSE

Part of the beauty of the Catholic experience is the "universality" at its heart. Catholic spirituality is traditional and contemporary, silent, spoken, or musical, and can be expressed individually and communally. Being Catholic naturally presumes a communal and liturgical dimension to the spiritual life, but from there the sky's the limit. If you are drawn to prayer that is structured, ancient, and devotional, or spontaneous and free flowing, the paths are well marked. If you have a clear sense of your spiritual direction, you can jump right in, and if you need help, spiritual guidance of many kinds is always available.

Starting over with a little help may make the most sense, particularly for those who find prayer a mysterious enterprise altogether or who have not fared well within the limitations of their present prayer practices. Sitting in on one evening of contemplative prayer, or spending an afternoon at a retreat center, or even visiting a relative who prays the rosary daily and asking for a prayer lesson implies no long-term commitment and can become the open door through which an enlivening new direction may be discovered.

In our final chapter we will be making our case for why a rational person in the twenty-first century would consider pitching his or her tent within the Catholic Church. It's a big world, and there are plenty of ways to find meaning in it. So why be Catholic?

EIGHT

Why Be Catholic?

Claire didn't think of herself as Catholic, quite frankly, until she was in her forties. She had been raised by Catholic parents, baptized as a baby, and even attended parochial schools for a while. But she decided early on that the "Catholic experiment" had proved unsuccessful. She spent most of her school years in trouble, and the Sunday church scene seemed byzantine. The Catholic identity just didn't stick to her life in any meaningful way, or so it seemed at the time. When she stopped going to church, her parents didn't object, and by the time she was out on her own, she had forgotten about the church altogether.

One failed marriage, a reluctant abortion, and three decades later, Claire was about as far from the church as she could imagine being. But still she found herself standing in a Catholic church again, waiting to speak to a priest. Her father had died, her mother was too distraught to take care of the arrangements, and Claire knew it was her father's wish to be buried with a Catholic funeral. She had never been in this particular building before, and she expected the priest to be hostile to her request, to point out that she had no right to ask anything from the church, considering her poor track record overall. She had come in expecting the roof to crash down on her and perhaps to be denied a hearing even on this difficult occasion. Though at this time in her life Claire was the successful owner of her own business, the idea of talking to a priest made her feel about twelve years old and oddly scared.

But nothing happened the way she had anticipated. The priest was young and gentle-spoken, not like the grouchy old pastor who was locked in her childhood memory. He was very sympathetic to her story, which was so unexpected that she found herself crying and talking for the next hour about the struggles of her life—things she certainly hadn't planned on saying, to a priest of all people! He asked her if she intended this to be a matter for confession; not really understanding what he meant, she nodded, and he gave her absolution. Absolution for *everything:* for all the failures and rotten decisions, for the fact that life hadn't turned out the way she had hoped, for all the ways that she and others had suffered as a result. Though Claire had often had regrets about the turns her life had taken, it had never occurred to her that there could be *forgiveness,* an end to the remorse and the responsibility, a way to move on and find healing and start over. This was an extraordinary liberty she had just been offered, and despite the pain of her present mission, Claire found herself glad and grateful to be standing in that church.

Later that week the funeral for her father was a moving and powerful experience, and Claire could not put it out of her mind. The event had drawn her in, and she felt like she wanted more of this in her life, whatever it was that she was becoming part of. She had taken communion at the funeral for the first time as an adult, and suddenly this action, which had always seemed meaningless, became significant and comforting in a way that echoed through her for days afterward. Without intending it, without even consciously choosing it, Claire found herself belonging in that place again and wanting to be there.

As incredible as it still seems to her a decade later, Claire returned to the church, body and soul, that winter. She even received training to become a eucharistic minister and to extend that opportunity of belonging to others. "Being Catholic is the bottom line for me now," she admits with great enthusiasm. "I didn't just come back to the church—I *am* the church. I won't give up my seat again."

CATHOLICS WHO RETURN

Claire is just one of the legion of Catholics who found themselves on the outside of the church for years and then made their way back. A majority of Catholics who abdicate their seat in the church do return at some point in their lives, and the route back is as varied as the reasons they left. Some come back to raise their children with a strong set of values. Others feel a void that could not be filled by relationships and creature comforts. Some report a specific spiritual need or lack of meaning that drew them back. Those who came from families with close ties to the church may eventually feel remorse about being away from the sacraments. Certain life events may precipitate a second look at the church: a family crisis or marriage breakdown, the birth of a child, moving to a new community, even having an explicitly religious experience.

Catholics who return cite certain environmental factors as very inviting. Parishes that exhibit a participatory style of leadership are attractive, as are those that offer varied worship experiences and programs aimed at the returnees' particular age group or life experience. Nothing beats a direct encounter with a warm and sympathetic representative of the church, like the one Claire had with the priest who arranged for her father's funeral. Parishes that advertise in the bulletin or even the newspaper that they welcome Catholics who have been away and have a support group for returnees are likely to regularly get returning Catholics.

Ray came back to the church through such a group at age thirty. From the time he knew he was gay in his teens, being Catholic had no longer seemed an option. His life took a dramatically new trajectory, away from his hometown, the confused response of his family members, and the religion that had always seemed to say "negative things about sex in general—and double that if you're homosexual." Ray moved to a gay-friendly city and found support for the person he understood himself to be in a strong community and life-giving relationships. Things were painful when he looked back, so he tried to keep his focus on the present and the future.

"Then the future got shaky," he says simply. "Friends got sick, people got scared, my family wasn't there for me. Yet God had always been there, as strange as that may seem. I never doubted God, and I always had a reliance on the sense of the sacred. I even used to light candles for friends in trouble, that sort of thing. I knew I wasn't alone, that ultimately there was love and acceptance."

Ray may not have attempted a return to the pews, however, if it hadn't been for the ad he saw in the Sunday newspaper: "It was this outrageous photo of Lucille Ball tasting something awful and making such a grimace! The headline read, 'Catholicism Leave a Bad Taste in Your Mouth? Come and Talk about It!' I had to laugh. I thought, *The people behind this can laugh at themselves. That's a good sign.*" So Ray attended the advertised meeting at that church. He found a group of Catholics both in and out of the church who listened without judgment, asked sympathetic questions, and invited each person to come to Mass that Sunday and sit in the pews together. When he showed up that week, Ray was surprised how many others from the group did too. They pointed at one another, teased, and confessed their nervousness. And afterward they went out for coffee and agreed they were more than a little homesick for the church. They decided to keep on coming back to the parish-sponsored meetings and to Mass. With a little support they began to think they could work out their differences.

Ray came back to the church because of an explicit invitation. Sometimes that can happen one-on-one, as when a friend or coworker collars a "lapsed" pal and makes an offer that can't be refused: "Come to the 5:00 PM jazz Mass at St. Rita's on Sunday, and stay for the wine and cheese!" For others the anonymous approach works better, especially if there's a chance to tell the story that led to departure and to get some validation for the reasons they've been away.

In Paul's case, no invitation was necessary for him to return— unless you count the hunger for God an invitation. He had exited the church in his teens and stayed away for fifteen years. Today he is a Roman Catholic priest. As he recalls his early childhood experiences of being Catholic: "It was a mixture of fun and fear. Things like choir, being an altar boy, the festivals and outings were fun. But Mass was a drag, as was catechism. The fear of everlasting damnation was very real and acted in my life like eerie background music of a movie that you know is going to get really scary."

When asked about the specific circumstances of his departure, he says: "Two things made me stop going to church. The first was that I began to see a real gap between what the priests preached and how they lived. It seemed that all the money that the church collected for charity just got pumped back into the church facility. I didn't see the church helping the poor; it just seemed like they were helping themselves.

"The second thing was a growing disbelief that condemnation could be so universal. Based on what I was hearing, hardly any- body was going to make it to heaven, and just about everybody was going to hell. If it were all true, my own growing sinfulness—I was passing through adolescence—would surely put me in the flames no matter how much I went to confession, so there seemed to be no point in continuing. But I really didn't think God would damn someone for eating a hot dog on a Friday. So the whole thing began to fall apart for me, and as I gained more freedom from my parents, I stopped going."

What could persuade a person with such an experience to rethink his relationship with the church? Paul felt a tug in the part of himself that never stopped being active even when his membership in the church lagged: "In my late twenties I sensed the need for spiritual development and felt a growing desire to know more about the mystery beyond the material world. My search took me to the Bible, where I experienced a kind of resonance with what I had come to know about the things I sought. Gathering with like-minded people led me first to Christianity and then back to Catholicism. The church, only a decade into the reforms of Vatican II, was a whole new ball game. I wanted to enter more deeply and become a part of what I believed would help others who, like myself, had been pushed away or scared away from God by their early experiences."

Those who do return to the pews may ask themselves: Has the church really changed so much since I've been gone to make "coming home" an option? Or have my own experience and expectations of the church changed as well? Paul admits he still struggles with some of the issues that drove him away as a kid: "The harsh conservatism of many church leaders still tends to discourage people who are not able to muster the kind of moral, emotional, social, economic, and intellectual assets that would raise them to what I see as sometimes unreasonably high standards. Also, the church still seems to spend much of its time, energy, and resources protecting the institution and guarding its entrances. It seems to me that the church sets up unnecessary obstacles that block the way of people seeking to move closer to God. I remain Catholic for the same reason I returned: I think I can make a difference. I believe God is calling me to be part of the force that is reforming the church and bringing it closer to what it's supposed to be."

Claire came back to the church to make a fresh start in her life. Ray returned for the sake of the community and its support. Paul felt a sense of mission and call to be the welcoming presence he hadn't experienced himself. They represent only three of the many reasons why Catholics who walked out one door came back through another after years of being away. They didn't return to a perfect church, but they found ways to make peace with the church's humanity and a place within it to belong, to give, and to receive.

HANGING ON TO YOUR ROOTS

Young people are considered to be almost an endangered species within traditional religious circles across the board. Our world is much more deeply influenced by the media than ever before, and the worldview they offer can be flashier and more appealing than the plain-speaking message of Christianity. In a culture that promises every material pleasure right now, why wait or deny yourself? For those just emerging into adulthood with newfound independence and personal power, it can be an overwhelming challenge to remain faithful to the simpler spiritual values learned when the world seemed smaller and was contained within the family circle. Yet many obviously do. How do they do it and why?

"My parents aren't what I would have called 'real religious,'" Amy confesses. "They took us to Mass on Sundays, and we prayed before meals and at bedtime when we were little. But we didn't talk about our faith or anything like that. It was just understood, like the cross hanging in the living room and the small sculpture of the Last Supper in the kitchen. They didn't make a big deal out of it, but in the background of every decision they made for us was this fidelity: to God and to love. Without a lot of pious drama, that was it."

Amy's parents stayed together through all the rough times in a marriage, even the nights when she heard them arguing through the walls of her bedroom and knew they weren't always perfectly happy with each other. "I never doubted that they loved us and they were committed to each other," Amy says, "even when money was tight and they were disappointed with the way things were going. But I wondered sometimes why they didn't just throw in the towel and go get what was missing someplace else. I knew a lot of kids whose parents did, and I felt instinctively like my parents were doing something 'Catholic' in insisting on working things out every step of the way."

In college lots of Amy's friends gave up on organized religion and tried alternative spiritual paths. Amy dutifully went with her crowd to the local Vedanta center to try meditation or to hear lectures on Buddhism or transcendental meditation. But she always came back convinced she'd had the same experiences and heard the same message before—at the Newman Center, where she attended the weekly folk Mass and signed up for an occasional half hour of adoration before the Blessed Sacrament. "Maybe it was less cool to do all this in church instead of with the swamis, but I had to admit it all pointed to the same thing," she says.

Today Amy has her own apartment, and on the wall of her bedroom is a small cross. In the main room is a portrait of Our Lady of Guadalupe. "Is it kitschy?" Amy says. "Probably. But these are just signs of something deeper that is true about who I am. Being Catholic is not something I need to advertise, but it's the grass I walk on. I hope it will keep me true, the way it kept my parents."

Megan's experience of growing up Catholic was a little different. "My parents were social-justice hippies," she observes warmly. "They were dragging me off to Peace Corps–type countries from the time I was old enough to get a passport. I remember losing a baby tooth while picketing a lab where bombs were made. And I protested racial injustice before I understood what it meant. My folks always equated being Catholic with being part of 'the cause.' It never occurred to me that you could just go to Mass on Sunday and be done with it."

This unusual childhood experience seemed very normal at the time. "The Berrigans, Dorothy Day, Mother Teresa—all their pictures hung on the fridge," Megan explains. "Dad called them 'the relatives,' and we thought of them as aunts and uncles of the cause, I guess. OK, I admit I came home a few times wanting something the other kids were talking about at school, like three hours of junk TV a night or Guess jeans. Sometimes I didn't really want to hear about the greenhouse effect; I just wanted to know why we couldn't have a bigger family car! But Mom wasn't rigid about this stuff. She'd explain to me about kids my age working in sweatshops and then tell me I could have any pair of jeans I wanted during back-to-school shopping. And in the end, I just couldn't let her buy the designer pants. I just couldn't be that big of a jerk."

Megan remains skeptical of what she calls "pew-sitting" Catholics. "Going to Mass is important to me, but it would seem phony if that's what being Catholic meant," she says. "I like to look at the stained-glass saints and think of them as 'the relatives' too, but I also feel like I can't let them down. We're part of this family tree that they lived and died for, and I'd like to think I have a part to play in that."

Amy and Megan both think of themselves as "lifer" Catholics, in it for the long haul because of the steadfast influence that religious faith had on their parents. They appreciate the values they were taught and seek to emulate them. They believe staying close to the church will get them where they hope to go as faithful adults.

STAYING FAITHFUL DESPITE OBSTACLES

David's relationship to the church is not as uniformly smooth as Amy's or Megan's, and he admits to having his issues with Catholicism. But these acknowledged patches of disagreement do not fray his overall connection to the church. David is a musician in his early thirties; he is married to a woman who is Protestant, and the subject of religion takes on a dynamic character as a result of the way his church distinguishes between him and his wife. "Hard lines are drawn around who's *in* and who's *out*," he declares. "When Jesus said, 'This is my body, which is given up for you' and 'This is my blood, which is shed for all,' I interpret this literally. Jesus invites everyone to Eucharist despite the fact that none of us deserve it; yet our human institutions are much less welcoming!"

It is not hard for David to list other policies of the church that are incongruous with his sense of justice. But he doesn't find it difficult to say why he remains Catholic despite these conflicts: "I meet many enlightened people in the church whose values are similar to mine. Although the official church position on these issues is antagonistic, I see God's will being done despite rigid policy." He has also visited other corners of organized religion and found strengths and faults everywhere he goes. In the end, he returns home to Catholicism. He explains the reason this way: "The Catholic Church still offers me a poetic form of worship that appeals to me strongly."

David is optimistic about where the church is heading through history. "I hope that inspired people within the church will listen to the Holy Spirit," he says, "and help drive reform from the inside. I believe that the Catholic Church represents an earnest interpretation of God's desires—as humans are best able to interpret them. Christianity has evolved slowly over two millennia and must continue to grow, or it will die. Jesus seems to promise that it will not die. So change is inevitable."

When asked what's best about being Catholic, David does not hesitate to reply: "Catholics acquire a strong sense of history and devotion through the Mass. When I visit churches that use a less structured form of worship, I miss this the most. Saying the familiar prayers again and again, each utterance calls my attention to different phrases, and I realize how rich Catholic liturgy is. I don't get that experience anywhere else.

"I like knowing that Catholics worldwide are on the same calendar, observing grief and redemption as a unit. If the church can represent God's desires for humanity, then it must also represent humanity's unifying desire for God. Few things on earth move in unison, internationally and across cultures. Although not all-inclusive as its name might suggest, the Catholic Church is the closest thing I know to a unified expression of Christianity. That excites me."

Richard, a businessman also in his thirties, shares with David an abiding enthusiasm and respect for the unity of the church. Before he broaches the subject of his faith, Richard wants his feelings about the church to be clear: "I am glad to be part of the church. The problems faced today don't affect my belief in Christ or make me doubt that things can be improved to better serve the church community." But he still feels free to express some concerns and to regret a perceived lack of communication between the hierarchy and the laity. Richard is a self-styled conservative in many ways, but he can't find it in his heart to be dogmatic and unquestioning about something as important as his faith. He would like to hear church leaders teach the truths of the faith more clearly and directly, which in his opinion is not happening enough. The real presence of Christ in the Eucharist at Mass is not emphasized very often, and other doctrines are still fuzzy in the minds of the faithful. He would like to see more religious education for adults rather than capitalizing on the religious formation of children. "I think people tend to get caught up more in church tradition than in faith," he says. "Faith should be emphasized first."

At the same time, Richard believes the hierarchy has to reconsider some of its hard-line organizational policies. "Priests should be allowed to marry if they choose," he states simply. "Making this a policy just because Christ wasn't married is not a good reason to ban marriage for all priests." Richard advocates an increased public presence in the church for women: "Women should be able to consecrate the Host and perform all sacraments." These are challenges the church has yet to face, and Richard has faith in the church's ability to meet them.

His appreciation for the Catholic tradition is much larger than his critique of it: "I like the Mass, the sacraments, the emphasis on community. I like the *idea* of the church hierarchy, the Vatican, pope, bishops, priests, and their connection to Peter and to Christ. I stay Catholic for the good things I see; it's a place where people can be closer to God. The church is a haven where we can be together, to worship and to strengthen our community. The more I feel a part of this community, the more I want to see the Catholic Church do God's work."

David and Richard view their religious faith primarily in terms of a personal choice for their own lives. For Jim, remaining faithful to his Catholic heritage as a father of three young girls involves what's best for the innocent lives dependent on his care. The clergy sex abuse scandals recently uncovered are at the top of the list of things that cause him to struggle in his relationship with the church. "I have no words to fully describe the pain, the sadness, and the anger I feel toward these perpetrators," he admits. "Yet I find my faith in the Catholic Church shaken more by those who covered up each and every incident. Those involved in the cover-up were probably very sane individuals motivated by the desire to maintain the power and position of the church, and perhaps their individual careers within the church. That hurts the most."

But on less specific issues, Jim finds other complaints in his local experience of the church: "I struggle every time I listen to our pastor water down his message on any given Sunday. I think, in many cases, he does not fully discuss moral truth for fear that he may offend one or more significant givers. That's hard to take."

Jim's dissatisfaction with certain aspects of church leadership does not threaten his overall commitment, however. How does he distinguish his faith from the matters that disappoint him? As he puts it: "I suggested to a good friend of mine (after his critical review of the church) that I feel it is important to separate the theology of the Catholic faith from the institution that runs it. Clearly, the human element of the church is flawed. Yet the theology remains intact. Our pastors do lack moral courage, at times. This is a human failing. Still, moral truth remains the foundation of the church. For me it's a comfort to know that our faith doesn't compromise moral truth to 'fit' the beliefs of each local congregation."

Jim shares with many Catholics the conviction that the "catholicity" of the church is its hallmark and its most attractive feature: "It is a real comfort to know and feel a connection with each and every Catholic across the globe. To be able to travel across the country and stop anywhere, anytime, at any Catholic church, attend Mass, and feel connected with that congregation is remarkable. The consistency of our faith and the ritual of the Mass, I believe, make that connection. Finally, I relish the opportunity to be part of the heritage and tradition of the church. In an era where secular culture and beliefs change daily, it's a real privilege to be part of an institution that has survived for over two thousand years."

FOLLOWING JESUS

Many people who remain active within the church are not there because of the church per se. Although not always articulated so plainly, the implication of religious faith is more than its outward trappings. More simply, the attraction is not the church: the pull is the One who is at the center of it all. For Elaine, a laywoman who works full-time as a pastoral associate in a Catholic parish, her dedication to the person of Jesus is what keeps her close to a church that often seems far from heaven. When asked what the best thing about being Catholic is, her response is passionate: "What a question! I guess the best thing is knowing who and what I am. I am a follower of Jesus Christ, and I am called to have that shape my life."

But why celebrate that identity in this particular context? She elaborates: "Why? I am reminded of Scripture: 'To whom else shall we go?' Yes, this is the faith that fed my ancestors for endless generations. Through it, God has kept us all alive and connected to one another. It feels like it's in my DNA. But it's more than just an inheritance for me. I love the image of God-in-Jesus and of life that I find in my church. There are principles for living here, and they are about love and forgiveness and living as a community. They are about experiencing God in creation and finding joy in all that is. These principles inform everything about my life and make it rich."

One might assume that Elaine has had a particularly easy relationship with the church, considering that she has chosen to make it her life's work. But when asked if she struggles with aspects of her church experience, she sighs and says: "Let me count the ways: The unchristian use of authority and power in the structure of the church bothers me. Our tradition sometimes traps us instead of giving life to us, as with women's limited role in the church, the limited promotion of lay leadership, the pyramid structure of power that Vatican II was supposed to change (but how often do we see this?), the unhealthy 'good old boy' network of clergy that protects itself instead of empowering others and the truth. These institutional structures are so often historically based, not theologically grounded."

When asked about other ways the church falls short of its vocation in the world, Elaine does not hesitate: "I am turned away from the lack of evangelization of church members (the 'full, conscious, active participation' the church calls for) and how much current church leadership seems to nurture this attitude. So many Catholics have a faith that isn't a personal relationship with God— it's an immature following of rituals based on a judgmental God who uses fear and guilt to induce obedience. I feel this is an insult to God in addition to the individuals involved. The great reforms and ideas of Vatican II are too often lost on people because those reforms haven't taken root in our parish communities and, too often, in our hearts. The teachings of Jesus Christ and how those can be embodied are beautiful and transforming. Too often Catholics are offered a dried-up faith that isn't relevant to their lives, and not enough passionate Catholics to help them find something more."

Elaine is dedicated to being one of those passionate Catholics who demonstrate the difference a profound and personal faith can make in a person's life. Far from being deterred or alienated by the conflicts she experiences in the present-day church, she finds in it all her purpose. "Without my Catholic faith shaping my life and bringing it to life," she explains, "I would be as shaky as . . . as . . . 'a fiddler on the roof.' I stay connected to Catholic friends and communities that share my vision of the church. The Catholic tradition gives me tools to understand God in my life. God works through my faith so that it gives me hope, helps me envision a world other than the one I see, and empowers me to live outside of myself. My faith makes my life . . . more meaningful." She smiles, adding, "The church also gives me a community of like-minded people to share the journey with. Those people are the closest thing to family I could have."

For Elaine, Jesus makes the ideal of the church worth fighting for. For Tom, a man in his fifties who has also lived close to his faith in the support of Catholic families as a speaker and discussion leader, Jesus is at the core of his work and his heart. He tells this story: "When I was in grammar school, I heard stories about how Communists would barge into schools in countries behind the Iron Curtain. They would grab a crucifix from the front of the room (much like the crucifix in front of my classroom), and they would urge all the kids to spit on the cross. The unasked question hung in the room: what would you do?

"I knew the correct answer: die rather than blaspheme the Lord. Yet I had a deep, hidden fear that in reality I'd be spitting away. At that point, I had little idea of the truths that cross represented. I was grateful Jesus was willing to die for me, but as to why, I just didn't 'get it.' Today is different. I believe the way of Jesus contains the central and sacred truths that can transform human life (my life) into eternal, divine life. I believe the Christian faith that has been handed down may have meandered in some strange ways, but at its core it carries within it a spiritual path and a way of living that reveals my true identity and leads to my destination: life in God. There is so much richness and depth to the faith that it takes a decision to be a disciple in order to 'get it.' We have to take on a whole new way of seeing in order to 'put on Christ' as St. Paul says. We have to enter into mysteries and paradoxes, one of which is turning to an all-too-fallible institution to access the authentic truths about all creation and our Creator."

Tom is thoughtful as well as honest about his own commitment: "If someone burst into my office today and told me to spit on a crucifix under pain of death, I'm still coward enough to secretly worry about my response. But I do try to live each day according to the spiritual truths that the Catholic Church holds as its legacy. I know that what that cross represents is indeed worth dying for, but even more important to me, worth living for—day by day by day."

It's both amusing and telling that Tom can go from an expression of the sublime significance of his faith to the somewhat ridiculous particulars of it without missing a beat. He recounts an especially bad recent experience with a visiting preacher at his church who went on and on "in a scolding tone, beyond thirty minutes" during Mass. "It seemed arrogant, insensitive, and torturous," Tom remembers. "Other parts of the Mass were mediocre at best. And then at communion, we sang, 'I myself am the bread of life. You and I are the bread of life.' And I was moved to a combination of repentance for my own arrogance and frustration and relief at my true identity—a member of the Body of Christ. I don't get that message anywhere else. I hear that I'm a consumer, that I deserve a break today, that I will only be happy with more, more, more, or that we need to bomb and attack other people to be secure. But I don't hear that I am the Body of Christ, broken and blessed, poured out and shared. And quite frankly, I need to hear that regularly because I'm a slow learner and a fast forgetter. That's why I need the church."

BANISHING THE "HAPPY CATHOLIC" IDEAL

What becomes clear after talking with involved and devout Catholics of every age group, political persuasion, and personal style is that the ideal of the "happy Catholic," out there dwelling in blissful contentment with every aspect of his or her life in the church, is misleading. A surprising percentage of the folks sitting in the pews (or even in the sanctuary) have been away from the church at some point in their lives. Others have arrived punctually every Sunday but not without some serious considerations and caveats. Some Catholics have broken the rules and found themselves at great odds with the teachings of the church. Finally, many of the staunchest Catholic adherents have concerns and bad experiences within their life in the church. But none of these things move these folks to sign off altogether and stay home or find a religious path elsewhere. For many, perhaps most, Catholics in the pews, finding a practical peace with the humanity of the church for the sake of its divine elements is a balance worth achieving. This often means making peace with our own humanity as well and accepting the reality that, like St. Paul, we aren't always the Christians we mean to be. As he says in Romans 7:19, "I do not do the good I want, but the evil I do not want is what I do" (NRSV).

It might surprise many of us to speak to our older Catholic family members, in an unguarded and undefensive moment, about their own struggles and disappointments with the church. Even though Grandma prays her rosary every afternoon, she may still shake her fist at the local bishop's latest fiscal decision. The woman who professed her vows with a religious community forty years ago loves her life as a sister and yet, without taking a breath, can recite five issues the church needs to reconsider. Catholic parents help their children learn their catechism by heart and do not feel they are being unfaithful when they explain to the kids that their own informed conscience, to which they are answerable, is a higher authority than the pope himself.

Being a faithful and loyal Catholic, in other words, is not incompatible with the idea of wrestling with and finding instances of dissent in matters that are not essential to the faith. If you have doubts about what the essential faith of the church is, get a copy of the Nicene Creed, the "profession of faith" we make at Mass, and read it carefully and prayerfully. It was written to capture the church's understanding of itself and of the revelation of God, Jesus, and the Holy Spirit. It is the gold standard of Catholic Christian belief. The rest of church tradition and teaching is built on this foundation. If we struggle with other aspects of church policy and practice, these concerns do not separate us from the faith of Jesus Christ. If we do not yet know something to be true as the church teaches it, we cannot give our testimony to it. Since the informed conscience is the highest authority to which we must answer, any matter of dissent is a call for further study, reflection, and prayer on the issues that give rise to the conflict. To such prayerful consideration belongs the future of the church, for every renewal and reform began with a movement in the hearts of the faithful. The fruits of this labor of love will sometimes be greater clarity and respect for the church's position and will on other occasions be an expansion or reconsidering of the teaching itself. But above all, as the church, together we will achieve the wisdom and understanding the Holy Spirit promises.

CHOOSING TO BE CATHOLIC TODAY

A conversation about the church, we might agree by now, is a lot more complicated than it looks at first glance. What do we mean by our use of the word *church,* and what do we want—or reject—when we take a stand in regard to the church? Protestant theologian Karl Barth liked to speak of the church as a great crater left by the impact of God's revealing word. (See his commentary on "Letter to the Romans," 1933.) He saw the church in a way that is more stark, powerful, and historically devastating than others might. But biblical scholar E. P. Sanders viewed the institutional reality of the church more skeptically. He observed that while Jesus proclaimed the coming of the kingdom, it was the church that arrived. (See *Jesus and Judaism,* Philadelphia: Fortress Press, 1987, 91.) Others might insist that Christianity is not a religion so much as a *faith* in a *person.* Such a person would certainly emphasize the call to follow Jesus as more critical than choosing a denominational "flavor." Many might agree with the assessment that Jesus is more essential than the religious practices that came after him. The story has been told of Edith Stein having to answer to her Jewish mother when she sought to convert to Catholicism and join the convent. Her mother did not lament the idea that her daughter had fallen in love, but that the object of her love was that particular man, Jesus.

For most Christians sincerely trying to live out their faith, this is what it comes down to: pledging our lives to the particular person of Jesus Christ. As Catholics, we commit to that pledge through our baptism and are sustained in that desire in our celebration of the Eucharist. As we've said, there are hundreds of reasons to refrain from receiving the Eucharist and only one reason to receive it: because Jesus has invited us to be there and to share in his life. In the centrality of this act, all other factors regarding church organization pale in significance.

Our unity around this table becomes the window through which we see ourselves as children of God, sisters and brothers in Christ, and bearers of the Holy Spirit. Nourished by this meal, we move outward to share the gospel in works of love, justice, peace, charity, faithfulness, forgiveness, and hope. It would be a paramount loss to ourselves and to the world if we allowed any secondary matter to keep us from our place at the table, which is our right according to our baptism and our greatest gift from the compassionate hands of Jesus.

This doesn't mean the pain or disharmony we may feel with specific teachings of the church or particular representatives of the institution will just go away. It does mean we have to decide to which we will assign more power: the pain of the past or the present call of the Lord. "See, now is the acceptable time; see, now is the day of salvation!" St. Paul urgently reminds us (2 Cor 6:2 NRSV). This is the hour in which we exercise our freedom, and no obstacle is great enough to keep us from Christ: "What will separate us from the love of Christ? Will anguish, or distress, or persecution, or famine, or nakedness, or peril, or the sword? No, in all these things we conquer overwhelmingly through him who loved us. For I am convinced that neither death, nor life, nor angels, nor principalities, nor present things, nor future things, nor powers, nor height, nor depth, nor any other creature will be able to separate us from the love of God in Christ Jesus our Lord" (Rom 8:35, 37–39 NAB). Either Paul is guilty of tremendous hyperbole here, or we can be reassured that all of the things that seem insurmountable between us and our unity in Christ are much more negotiable than we thought.

Robert Frost wrote in his stirring poem "The Death of the Hired Man": "Home is the place where, when you have to go there, / They have to take you in." Members of a family, no matter how fractious their relationships may be, belong to one another in irrevocable ways. In that sense, all baptized Catholics can think of the church as the place where we cannot be denied entrance, no matter "what we've done or failed to do," as we pray at the beginning of Mass. This implies that the door of the church is one that can never be closed and bolted behind us. If we want to be there, our right to belong is guaranteed.

Some folks have been away from the church for a quarter century or twice that amount of time. Chances are, the church to which they return will seem surprisingly new. That may be confusing and difficult at first. But for others, especially those who have been gone for only a few years, the church they return to might seem maddeningly unchanged. In any case, it would be unrealistic to assume that one could ever return to the church without conflict and contradiction being part of the picture. This is not an institution handed to us on a celestial platter and governed by angelic beings. What may be most challenging for many who return to the church after an absence of any length is that the sources of tension or disagreement are still where you left them.

It would be dishonest for anyone to promise you that a future relationship with the church would be free from the strife involved in the old one. When a separated couple comes back together for a second try, what caused hardship between the couple in the past is bound to be a factor in the future. But what *may* have changed is the couple's willingness to talk about the trouble, and they may have a renewed commitment to work things through. Finding a community that is not afraid of honest dialogue will go far toward making sure that past issues do not remain submerged like land mines in the future. Without that dialogue, we are all the poorer. Engaged in that conversation, we ensure that none of the gifts of the Body of Christ will be lost, to the church or to one another.

Epilogue for the Unpersuaded

We write this epilogue knowing that not everyone who has left the church or is struggling to remain within it will be able to make the journey of faith with the Catholic Christian community. Some of you may have been given this book by a friend or family member who hoped it would change your mind about the church. You may have read it half hoping for a reason to make that choice yourself or to confirm for yourself that such a choice, in your case, is impossible. We are grateful you took the time to consider this issue with us and chose to give your attention to this conversation. We pray for your healing and wholeness, and ask God's mercy "for what we have done and what we have failed to do" as your sisters and brothers in Christ. We hope you can make peace with your past association with the church and find a life-giving way to sustain you on the road ahead. And if we do meet again further down the road, we will welcome a renewal of this relationship.

May God bless and guide you on your journey!

Resources

INFORMATION ON CATHOLICISM

For a good general introduction to Catholicism, consider *Invitation to Catholicism: Beliefs, Teachings, Practices,* by Alice Camille (Chicago: ACTA Publications, 2001), which takes the reader through a tour of the Catholic faith. Not your mother's catechism, this book seeks to present what is "good, beautiful, and true" at the heart of the Catholic worldview.

Unlike most catechisms, which start with doctrine, Andrew M. Greeley's *The Great Mysteries: An Essential Catechism* (New York: Seabury Press, 1976) starts with human experience to ground doctrine and beliefs in people's lives.

One of the most accessible general reference works on Catholicism is *The HarperCollins Encyclopedia of Catholicism,* edited by Richard P. McBrien (New York: HarperCollins, 1995). Perhaps the best introduction to the sacraments is Joseph Martos's *Doors to the Sacred: A Historical Introduction to Sacraments in the Catholic Church* (Liquori, Mo.: Liquori/Triumph, 2001).

THE LITURGY OF THE HOURS ONLINE

Several Web sites offer versions of the Liturgy of the Hours you can follow at your computers. Check out www.universalis.com, www.oremus.org, and www.liturgyhours.org.

INFORMATION ON RETREATS

For retreats and information about them, see *Catholic America: Self-Renewal Centers and Retreats,* by Patricia Christian-Meyer (Santa Fe, N.Mex.: John Muir Publications, 1989).

You can find Sacred Space, an online prayer and retreat Web site produced by the Jesuits of Ireland, at www.jesuit.ie/prayer. As of this writing, other online retreats are available at www.creighton .edu/CollaborativeMinistry/cmo-retreat.html; www.thedome.org/ SpiritQuest/Retreat/Lectio/; and www.stgertrudes.org (click on "Online Retreats").

RESOURCES FOR ALIENATED CATHOLICS AND PARISHES REACHING OUT TO THEM

Several books address alienated Catholics themselves. An especially helpful one is *Faith Rediscovered: Coming Home to Catholicism,* by Lawrence Cunningham (New York: Paulist Press, 1987). It "is addressed to those who have come back to the practice of the faith or are at least open to that idea." Less a how-to manual and more a source of encouragement, Cunningham's book tries to "set out the basic faith of Catholics and, in the process, to insist that persons who want to return are welcome; their presence is desired; their absence has been felt."

Two excellent volumes that help parishes carry out programs to assist alienated Catholics are *Catholics Coming Home: A Journey of Reconciliation: A Handbook for Churches Reaching Out to Inactive Catholics,* by Carrie Kemp and Donald Pologruto (San Francisco:

HarperSanFrancisco, 1990) and *Catholics Can Come Home Again! A Guide for the Journey of Reconciliation with Inactive Catholics,* by Carrie Kemp (New York: Paulist Press, 2001). As the late Bishop Raymond Lucker has said, "Carrie Kemp has devoted much of her life to 'the seekers,' who for various reasons have left the church, but deep down in their hearts long for the sacraments and wait for an invitation to talk." These books not only provide complete guides for parishes designing outreach programs, they also make valuable reading for alienated Catholics themselves.

PROGRAMS FOR RETURNING CATHOLICS

The North American Forum on the Catechumenate (NAFC) has promoted the Re-Membering Church program, and the Paulists offer Landings and Catholics Coming Home. These programs may be available in the diocese where you live. Call the NAFC (its Web site is www.naforum.org) or the Paulist Fathers (online at www.paulist.org) to find out. The Cincinnati Franciscans also have a Web site (http://oncecatholic.org) that provides multiple resources for Catholics who have left the church.

AIDS TO READING AND REFLECTING ON SCRIPTURE

For those who are attending daily Mass during the week and want to reflect more personally on the Gospel reading for the day, a handy one-volume resource is *Between Sundays: Daily Gospel Reflections and Prayers,* by Paul Boudreau (Mystic, Conn.: Twenty-Third Publications, 2001), which provides a verse from the Gospels for each weekday of the year, along with a conversational and often humorous reflection, prayer, and suggested activity with which to respond.

For Sunday Mass preparation many parishes make available the monthly serial *Exploring the Sunday Readings,* by Alice L. Camille, a user-friendly encounter with Scripture. If your parish doesn't supply it, you can order a personal subscription from Twenty-Third Publications (www.twentythirdpublications.com). Since the Sunday readings are repeated every three years, a three-year supply of Sunday reflections is brought together in the one-volume *God's Word Is Alive! Entering the Sunday Readings,* by the same author (Mystic, Conn.: Twenty-Third Publications, 1998).

For a very readable commentary on every book of the Bible, consult *The Collegeville Bible: Based on the New American Bible with Revised New Testament Commentary,* edited by Dianne Bergant and Robert J. Karris (Collegeville, Minn.: Liturgical Press, 1989).

PEOPLE WHO MAY PROVIDE GUIDANCE

Some dioceses have hotlines offering information to Catholics who have been away from the church. Call the chancery office of your diocese to obtain that number. You may prefer to start by meeting with a representative of the church at a local parish or one that has been recommended to you. You may choose to speak with a priest, or you may feel more comfortable talking with a lay pastoral associate, religious sister or brother, or deacon. You may also wish to talk to a Catholic friend or relative whom you trust and admire, who will be sympathetic to your situation, and with whom you can have an open conversation. If you are looking for a spiritual director, you can contact Spiritual Directors International (online at www.sdiworld.org). Any of these options will help you to decide when and where to take the next step in your relationship with the church.

SOME IDEAS ABOUT WHAT TO DO NEXT

In *Catholics Can Come Home Again!* (see "Resources for Alienated Catholics and Parishes Reaching Out to Them," earlier in the resources), Carrie Kemp provides some very helpful suggestions for Catholics who are angry or inactive, or who have been hurt by the church. Some of her recommendations—like hearing an apology from the church, finding a church representative who will listen to you, and searching out a welcoming and comfortable worshiping community—we have mentioned.

We also heartily commend to you another piece of Kemp's advice: to remember that as a baptized Catholic, you are a member of the church. God's love for you and invitation to respond to how God is working in your life come as a gift, not something you have to earn.

Besides starting a conversation with a trustworthy representative of the church, we also echo Kemp's suggestion to take part in some kind of solid adult education program to update your knowledge of the church and its beliefs in order to inform your faith. If you have not already done so, and if you feel ready at this point, try to get into the habit of regular prayer. Pray for yourself, the church, and for all who need guidance and help.

Do one thing at a time. Take small steps. Don't think you have to resolve *all* your problems with the church, or lots of them, at once or that you need to rush back into participation in the church as fast as you can. Discern what is separating you from the church. Talk about it with someone. Read and educate yourself. Affirm what you want from the church. Explore what participation in the church means and how you might resume your participation. Let God guide you to the place that is right and comfortable and just challenging enough to help you grow as a follower of Jesus Christ.